Date Night

Meals to Make Together
for a Romantic Evening

SLOANE TAYLOR

Date Night Dinners
Sloane Taylor

Toque & Dagger Publishing

Issued by Toque & Dagger Publishing, June 2018

ISBN: 978-1-7323635-2-6

Editor: Sloane Taylor
Interior Book Design: HL Carpenter
Cover Photo: Chris Pavesic

For Studs who is always there for me during the good and the bad.

You are my hero.

ACKNOWLEDGEMENTS

This book would never have happened if it were not for the amazing talents, support, and extreme patience of HL Carpenter and Chris Pavesic. My heartfelt thanks, ladies, for all you have done for me. You are the best.

To my British buddies Carol Browne and Susan Lodge and my Canadian cohort Sharon Ledwith for suggesting the conversion chart included in this book and guiding me through the metric system. A huge thanks, my friends, from your favorite Yank.

I Blame Uncle Steve

My obsession with cooking is his fault. No denying it. He was a carpenter until the Army sent him an invitation to join their illustrious ranks. He did and was made a cook. Go figure. Until then he had no clue about kitchen work, but he soon learned and loved his job. Fast forward to me age five. This quiet mountain of a man sat me in a chair close to the stove where he created magic with the merest of supplies. He was patient and answered every dumb question I asked while he encouraged me to toss in a handful of chives, parsley, or whatever else was available. He made cooking interesting and fun. Watching and working with my favorite uncle was a wonderful experience I cherish.

Time passed and I setup my own household. No longer did I have the ease of single dish prep. I had to concoct the *entire* meal and was expected to cook *many* entire meals. Fear struck so I beelined to the store and stocked up on cookbooks. And that led to frustration. All those delicious sounding recipes left it up to me to decide what to serve with them. Beans or peas? Fried or boiled potatoes? To salad or not. You get the idea. We're not talking *Haute cuisine*, but a clue or two from those big-buck chefs, whose books I paid dearly for, would sure have helped. And that's why I took matters into my own hands and wrote a cookbook with full menus minus desserts. I don't bake and my family is grateful since my creations are horrible.

Back to hands, I use mine for most meal prep instead of spoons and spatulas. Therefore, I work with big pots, pans, and bowls. That means more washing by hand, but everything stays in the container and I have room to work comfortably with the ingredients instead of them flying all over the counter.

We're cooking here not baking, so no need to be precise. Change measurements to suit your taste. You love garlic – toss in more. Pepper isn't your thing – leave it out. Make these recipes your own. Side dishes and beverages are suggestions not a rule of thumb. Those recipes are found in the Veggies section or Salads, Sauces, Sides, & Extras section at the back of the book.

So grab your partners and don your aprons. Crack open a bottle of your favorite wine! Let's take a giant step forward to ease the burden of overworked women and bring romance back into our lives with meals to make together for a romantic evening.

May you enjoy all the days of your life filled with laughter and seated around a well laden table!

Sloane

Contents

Meat

Beef

Pork

Poultry

Fish & Seafood

International Dishes

Salads, Sauces, Sides, & Extras

Salads

Sauces

Sides

Extras

Veggies

Bonus Content

MEAT

This easy meal is a favorite of Studs, especially since leftovers make great sandwiches. I think you and yours will enjoy it, too. It's also a bare hands-on prep. Dive in with your partner and have fun.

Serve with Mashed Potatoes, Snazzy Sliced Tomatoes, and Red Wine – Merlot.

BARBEQUED MEATLOAF

2 slices white bread torn into bits
½ cup (120ml) milk
1½ lbs. (750g) ground chuck
½ lb. (230g) ground pork*
3 tbsp. (60ml) onion, chopped fine
1 egg, lightly beaten
Scant ½ cup (120ml) barbeque sauce

*If you prefer not to use pork, increase ground chuck to 2 lbs. (900g).

Preheat oven to 350° F (180°C).

Soak bread crumbs in milk 5 minutes. Drain excess liquid.

In a medium-sized bowl, combine all ingredients. Mix well with your hands, then shape into a loaf.

Place loaf in a nonstick pan. Bake 1 hour 15 minutes. Carefully drain off accumulated juices. Allow loaf to cool 5 minutes, then slice into the required number of serving pieces.

Leftovers freeze well. Cover in cling wrap and then refrigerate. It's much easier to slice the meatloaf after it has chilled. The next day I slice the meat into sandwich size pieces, then cling wrap them in pairs for later.

When the cold weather hits this is a great recipe to warm you. Don't worry about alcohol content. It cooks away and leaves behind a rich taste to enhance the meat.

Serve with Egg Noodles, Snazzy Tomato Salad, and Red Wine – Cabernet Sauvignon.

BEEF BRAISED in STOCK & RED WINE

1 tsp. (5ml) garlic, pressed
1 tsp. (5ml) dried oregano
Freshly ground pepper to taste
8 – 10 half-inch (1.25cm) pieces of bacon
3 lbs. (1.5kg) English cut or rump roast
3 tbsp. (42g) butter
1 tbsp. (15ml) olive oil
½ cup (60g) onions, coarsely chopped
¼ cup (30g) carrots, coarsely chopped
¼ cup (30g) celery, coarsely chopped
½ cup (120ml) dry red wine
2 cups (500ml) beef stock
1½ cups (350ml) canned diced tomatoes, drained
1 bay leaf

Preheat oven to 350° F (180°C).

Mix garlic, oregano, pepper, and bacon together. Make deep incisions in beef and insert bacon.

In a heavy skillet combine 1 tbsp. butter with olive oil over medium-high heat. Brown beef evenly on all sides.

Melt remaining butter over moderate heat in a Dutch oven. Be careful not to let it burn while you place prepped onions, carrots, and celery on a cutting board and chop them together until fine. Stir this mixture into the Dutch oven. Stir frequently for 10 minutes or until veggies are soft and lightly colored. Place the browned beef on top.

Discard most of the fat from the skillet. Pour in wine and boil briskly over high heat, stirring and scraping in browned fragments that cling to the bottom and sides of the pan. When the wine's reduced to ¼ cup (60ml), add it to the Dutch oven with beef stock, chopped tomatoes, and bay leaf. The liquid should come about a third of the way up the side of the beef. Add more stock if necessary. Bring to a boil over high heat, cover tightly, and braise in the middle of the oven for 2 hours or until meat is tender when pierced with the tip of a sharp knife.

Next, and this is really important, especially if you're cooking on your own. Pour yourself a glass of red wine, grab a good book, and read for the duration of the cooking time. You deserve it.

Transfer meat to a cutting board, tent with foil, and let rest 10 minutes.

Strain sauce through a fine sieve into a serving bowl, press hard on the vegetables to extract all their juice. Skim off as much fat as possible.

Egg Noodles
Follow package directions to cook. If the noodles are done before you're ready, drain them in a colander and set the lid on top to keep them warm.

REMEMBER: all noodles/pasta can easily be re-warmed by pouring hot water over them before serving.

To serve, scoop noodles onto dinner plates. Lay slices of meat alongside, overlapping each other. Top with a hearty serving of sauce.

Don't worry about the quantity if you and your favorite partner are the only ones at the dinner table. Slice off just the amount of roast you think you'll eat, and freeze the rest in the sauce. It's great for those days when you're too busy to bother with more work.

Your stove and countertop will be a mess from boiling down the wine. No problem! Grab the glass cleaner. A few sprays and it wipes right up.

Beef is a favorite with Studs and most men. Beef on bones is like manna from heaven to them. Must be something carried over from caveman days. Here's an easy dinner that will tame the beefaholic in your life.

Serve with Boiled Potatoes, Fresh Green Beans, and Red Wine – Pinot Noir.

BRAISED SHORT RIBS

2 – 3 lbs. (1 – 1.5kg) beef short ribs, cut into 2 inch (5cm) or so pieces
Freshly ground pepper to taste
½ cup (60g) flour
½ tsp. (2.5ml) thyme
2 tbsp. (30ml) lard or solid shortening
2 medium onions, chopped
½ cup (60g) carrot, chopped

1 tbsp. (15ml) garlic, pressed
1 cup (250ml) beef stock
2 small bay leaves
1 tbsp. (30ml) Worcestershire sauce

Preheat oven to 325° F (160°C).

Pat ribs dry. Grind pepper over meat. Pour flour and thyme into a paper bag. Add 2 – 4 ribs at a time. Shake bag gently to coat meat. Remove ribs and set on a large plate. Continue until all ribs are coated.

Melt lard or shortening in a Dutch oven over medium-high heat until it shimmers. Carefully add ribs and brown them on all sides. Don't crowd the pan. Best to brown meat in batches so the cooking temperature remains constant. Return ribs to the plate. Lower heat to medium.

Add onions and carrots to the same pot. Sauté until onions are soft and transparent. Add garlic. Cook 45 – 60 seconds.

Stir in stock. Bring to a boil over high heat. Scrape in any brown bits clinging to the bottom and sides of the pan.

Reduce heat to medium. Stir in remaining ingredients.

Nestle ribs in pan and bring to a boil. Cover and then place in oven. Braise ribs for 1½ hours or until meat shows no resistance when pierced with the tip of a sharp knife.

Arrange ribs on a clean platter and tent with foil to keep them warm.

Strain braising liquid through a fine sieve into a saucepan. Press down hard on vegetables to extract juices. Discard vegetables. Skim off surface fat.

Bring pan to a hard boil. Cook 2 – 3 minutes to intensify flavor.

Pour sauce into a gravy boat and serve alongside ribs.

Romance can happen when you least expect it. Yes, even if cheeseburgers are on the menu. Combine this dinner with your favorite dessert and DVD for a wonderful stay-in evening.

Serve with Homemade Fries, Tomato & Cucumber Salad, Sautéed Mushrooms, and Cold Beer.

CHEESEBURGERS SLOANE STYLE

¼ lb. (115g) ground chuck per person
¼ lb. (115g) ground sirloin per two people
2 dashes Worcestershire sauce per patty
1 egg per 1½ lbs. (750g) meat, lightly beaten
2 tbsp.(30ml) fresh chives, snipped or 1 tbsp. (15ml) dried
1 hard roll per person
1 tbsp. (15ml) olive oil per roll
Slices of your favorite cheese

Combine meat, Worcestershire sauce, egg, and chives in mixing bowl. When mixture is well combined, break off clumps and form into balls. Set them onto waxed paper, then cover with another sheet of waxed paper. Use the bottom of a cake plate or large soup bowl to press the meat into a patty the thickness you like. Refrigerate until ready to fry.

Heat a frying pan or grill pan on medium-high heat. You'll know it's ready when you sprinkle a little water in the pan and the droplets dance.

Split rolls in half lengthwise. Brush oil on both insides. Lay oiled side in pan. Carefully toast then remove to dinner plates.

Fry patties in same pan until done to your preference. Be sure to turn only once.

Spoon a few mushrooms on burger. Lay cheese on top a minute or two before burgers are done cooking.

To serve, dress the burgers with ketchup, mustard, mayo, lettuce, onion, and tomato.

When the temps turn to freezing here in the Midwest I use the oven not only to enjoy the extra warmth, but also the marvelous aromas this recipe provides. These leftovers are excellent for another dinner or lunch. It freezes beautifully.

**Serve with Asian Salad, French Bread,
and Red Wine – Cabernet Sauvignon.**

DAMNED GOOD POT ROAST

1 clove garlic, pressed
1 tsp. (5ml) dried oregano
½ tsp. (2.5ml) lemon pepper
3 – 3½ lb. (1.5 – 1.25kg) boneless chuck roast
3 tbsp. (15ml) olive oil
1½ cups (350ml) beef stock, possibly more
1 medium onion, quartered
5 red potatoes, quartered
15 mini carrots
2 tsp. (10ml) cornstarch
¼ cup (60ml) beef stock

Preheat oven to 325° F (160°C).

Combine garlic, oregano, and lemon pepper to form an herb paste. Rub evenly over the meat.

Heat olive oil in a Dutch oven on medium-high. Once the oil shimmers carefully brown roast on all sides.

Pour in beef stock until it is half way or so up the meat. Add onion. Cover and bake 1 hour 45 minutes.

Spread potatoes and carrots around the meat. Add more stock if the pan looks too dry. Roast another 30 minutes or until vegetables are tender.

Remove meat and vegetables to a serving platter. Keep warm under foil while you prepare the gravy.

Strain liquid into a bowl or measuring cup. Skim off any fat. Return liquid to pot and heat on medium. Stir cornstarch into remaining stock. Pour into the simmering liquid. Increase heat and boil mixture 1 minute or until thickened, stirring constantly.

Cut roast into hunks. Set on individual plates or a serving platter. Circle meat with veggies. Serve the gravy on the side. French bread is marvelous for dipping!

Splurge this weekend with an eye of round roast cooked to perfection and all the tasty fixings. The beautiful aroma will draw your partner to the kitchen ready to help prepare dinner even if it's only to open and pour the wine.

Serve with Mashed Potatoes, Sautéed Broccoli, and Red Wine – Valpolicella.

EYE of ROUND ROAST with SAUCE

2¼ – 3 lb. (1 – 1.5kg) eye of round roast
2 tbsp. (30ml) olive oil
1 cup (250ml) beef stock

Remove meat from refrigerator 1 – 2 hours before cooking. Meat needs to be almost room temperature for this dish to work.

Preheat oven to 325° F (160°C).

Heat olive oil in a skillet set over medium-high heat until it shimmers. Using tongs or wooden spoons, brown the meat on all sides. Line a roasting pan with aluminum foil. Be sure to hang it a little over pan sides. Lay beef on foil. Pour stock into bottom of the pan, not over the meat.

Topping
4 tbsp. (60ml) mustard, either yellow or Country Dijon
2 lg. garlic cloves, pressed
¼ cup (30g) fresh parsley, chopped or 1 tbsp.(15ml) dried
Freshly ground pepper to taste

Mix above ingredients in a small bowl. Spread over the top and a little on the sides of the beef.

Roast in oven for 1 hour or until 140° F on a meat thermometer. Don't overcook or the meat will be tough. Check the liquid level and add more stock if it runs dry or the pan will burn. When meat is cooked, remove from oven, set on a cutting board and tent with foil to keep warm.

Sauce
¼ cup (60ml) dry red wine
1 cup (250ml) beef stock
1 tbsp. (15ml) red currant or seedless raspberry jelly
1 tbsp. (15ml) butter

Time to deglaze the roasting pan. It's easy and requires little effort.

Carefully remove foil from pan and discard.

Place pan over a burner set on medium. Add red wine. Turn heat to medium-high. Pour in stock. Boil until sauce has reduced to half while scraping in anything that clings to the bottom and sides of the pan.

Remove pan from the heat and swirl in butter. Keep sauce warm on very low heat while you carve the roast.

To serve, arrange pieces on individual plates or a platter. Dribble sauce over meat to moisten. Serve extra sauce on the side.

If you have leftovers, freeze the meat and sauce separately.

Grilled or stovetop, skirt steak is a dinner you will enjoy. This is not the tenderest cut of meat, but it is tasty when prepared the right way. There are two cuts, inside and outside. The inside is the better cut therefore a little more expensive. Be careful not to confuse skirt steak with flank steak. They are distinctly different and from different areas of the cow. Skirt comes from the plate while flank is cut nearer the animal's rear quarter.

Serve with Twice Baked Potatoes, Broccoli Florets, Sautéed Mushrooms, and Red Wine – Beaujolais.

MARINATED SKIRT STEAK

1 – 1½ lb. (450 – 750kg) skirt steak
½ cup (120ml) olive oil, maybe a little more
1 lime or ½ lemon, squeezed
2 gloves garlic, pressed or chopped fine
1 shallot, chopped
Freshly ground pepper to taste

Combine all ingredients in a plastic bag. Set bag in refrigerator for 1 – 5 hours.

Heat a grill pan or heavy skillet to medium-high. You'll know the temperature is right when water droplets sprinkled across the pan sizzle and evaporate instantly.

Remove steak from marinade and lay in hot pan. Discard marinade. Grill meat 3 minutes per side. Longer cooking will create tough and chewy meat.

Transfer steak to a cutting board and drape with aluminum foil. Let rest 5 minutes.

To serve, slice meat thin against the grain.

This recipe may also be cooked on an outdoor grill preheated to medium-high. Follow the cooking directions as listed above.

This is an elegant dinner with marvelous flavors that is easy to prepare. On a tight schedule? Most of this meal can be assembled in advance. Look for the ** in the instructions for the stopping point. Continue cooking on the day you wish to serve. I suggest you make extras and freeze them for future use.

Serve with Roasted Potatoes, Fresh Green Beans, Sautéed Mushrooms, and White Wine – Riesling.

MOCK CHICKEN LEGS

Use equal amounts of the three meats. If you are anti-veal, the beef and pork alone are still great. Increase their amounts to 1½ lbs. (750g) each.

1 lb. (450g) eye of round or other high quality beef roast, cut into 2 inch (5cm) cubes
1 lb. (450g) pork tenderloin, cut into 2 inch (5cm) cubes
1 lb. (450g) veal shoulder, cut into 2 inch (5cm) cubes
3 eggs
Freshly ground pepper to taste
1½ (160g) cups seasoned bread crumbs, possibly more

Olive oil
Skewers 6 – 8 inches (15 – 20cm) long

Alternate the meat cubes as you skewer them. Set aside on waxed paper.

**Stop here if you plan to cook the legs another day. If you made extras, this is the time to freeze them. Lay the skewers on a cookie sheet. Cover with cling wrap and refrigerate.

On the day of serving, combine eggs and pepper in a shallow bowl. Dip the skewers, one at a time, into the mixture. Roll in the bread crumbs then set them back onto the waxed paper. Refrigerate for at least ½ hour to set the coating.

Preheat oven to 350° F (180°C).

Heat ½ inch (1.25cm) olive oil in a frying pan. When the oil shimmers, carefully put in a few skewers and brown well on all sides. As they are cooked set them into a baking dish, stacking the skewers is fine.

Cover the dish and bake for 1 – 1 ½ hours or until fork tender.

Do *NOT* add any liquid to the meat. This dish produces its own fantastic sauce.

Be sure to serve fresh Italian or French bread with this dinner. You won't want to leave a drop of sauce in your bowl. Make the full recipe even if it is just two of you. Leftovers freeze well.

Serve with Egg Noodles, Tossed Salad, and Red Wine – Pinot Noir.

ONE POT BEEF STEW

5 tbsp. (75ml) olive oil, plus more as needed
1 lg. onion, chopped
8 sprigs fresh thyme or 1 tsp. (5ml) dried
4 lg. cloves of garlic, pressed
16 oz. (450g) mini bello mushrooms, halved
¾ tsp. (3.75ml) dry mustard
Freshly ground pepper to taste
2 lbs. (1kg) sirloin, remove fat and cut into chunks
4 tbsp. (60ml) red wine vinegar
2 tbsp. (30ml) tomato paste
3 cups (750ml) beef stock
2 tbsp. (30ml) sour cream – make them healthy ones

Heat 2 tbsp. (30ml) oil in a Dutch oven over medium heat until the oil shimmers. Add onions and thyme. Cook until onions are translucent, 5 – 7 minutes. Add garlic and sauté for 30 – 60 seconds. Scrape this combination into a bowl and set aside.

Heat pan again and then add 1 tbsp. oil. Stir in mushrooms and sauté until soft. Remove to same bowl as onions.

Add remaining oil to the same pan and heat on medium-high until the oil sizzles. Sprinkle dry mustard, then pepper on steak chunks. Brown meat on all sides. Set chunks in a bowl with other ingredients.

On medium heat, pour red wine vinegar into pan. Add tomato paste and blend in. Mix beef stock and sour cream in a small bowl, then add to pan. Bring to a simmer while stirring to make a fairly smooth broth. Add meat and other cooked ingredients. Heat through while stirring often.

Egg Noodles
Cook per package directions. If the noodles are done before the stew, drain them in a colander and set the pot or lid over the top to keep them warm.

REMEMBER: all noodles/pasta can easily be re-warmed by pouring hot water over them before serving.

To serve, scoop egg noodles into soup/salad bowls. Spoon hearty portions of stew on top.

Ribs are always welcomed in our household, even when we're knee deep in snow. Unable to reach the grill? No problem. Your oven will do just fine.

Serve with Boiled Potatoes, Tomato and Cucumber Salad, and Ice Cold Beer.

COUNTRY RIBS with BARBEQUE SAUCE

2 – 3 lbs. (1 – 1.5kg) country style pork ribs, preferably on the bone
5 sprigs fresh thyme or ½ tsp. (2.5ml) dried
1 cup (250ml) chicken stock, possibly more
1 bottle your favorite barbeque sauce

Preheat oven to 325° F (160°C).

Place ribs in an ovenproof dish in a single layer. Pour in a ½ inch (1.25cm) of stock or slightly more. Cover tight with aluminum foil and bake 45 minutes.

Discard cover. Slather on barbeque sauce and roast another 15 minutes.

Check if meat is done by inserting the tip of a sharp knife close to the bone. You should not see any pink.

REMEMBER – meat continues to cook for a short time after it is removed from the oven.

Serve with plenty of sauce on the side.

Once in a great while I'm compelled to cook a Sunday afternoon sit-down dinner like the one mom used to make. These aren't her recipes, but they are close. I hope you enjoy them as much as we do.

Serve with Mashed Potatoes, Sautéed Broccoli, Homemade Applesauce, and White Wine – Chardonnay.

BRAISED PORK LOIN

3 – 4 lb. (1.5 – 2kg) boneless pork loin
3 tbsp. (45ml) lard or solid shortening
2 med. onions, peeled and sliced
1 lg. garlic clove, sliced thin
2 med. carrots, scraped and chopped
1 cup (250ml) dry white wine
½ cup (120ml) chicken stock
¾ tsp. (3.75ml) dried thyme
½ tsp. (2.5ml) marjoram
½ tsp. (2.5ml) paprika
Freshly ground pepper to taste

Preheat oven to 350° F (180°C).

Pat roast dry with paper towels. Melt lard in a Dutch oven over medium-high heat. Add pork and brown on all sides, 17 – 20 minutes. Adjust heat so as not to burn any part of the roast.

Set meat on a plate. Reduce heat to medium. Sauté onions until they are soft and translucent, 5 – 7 minutes. Stir in garlic and cook 1 minute.

Add remaining ingredients to pot and bring to a boil. Return roast to pot along with any accumulated juices on plate. Cover tightly and braise in the center of the oven for 1½ hours or until a sharp knife inserts easily.

Set roast on a cutting board and tent with foil. Skim fat from the braising liquid. Strain the liquid and vegetables through a sieve, pressing down hard with the back of a spoon to extract as much juice as possible before discarding pulp.

Carve pork into serving slices and lay them on a platter. Moisten meat with a little sauce. Pour the remainder in a gravy boat and serve on the side.

Here is a unique method to bake a ham, and it sure is delicious. It's also perfect for dinner parties. Simply increase the size of the ham and dough. Your guests will love it.

Serve with Scalloped Potatoes, Candied Orange Carrots, Asian Salad, and White Wine – Chardonnay.

HAM BAKED in BREAD

3 – 5 lb. (1.5 – 2.5kg) ham, I use Kentucky Legend. It's excellent, but this recipe works for all boneless hams
2 tubes prepared pizza dough found in the refrigerated section of the grocery store
½ cup (120ml) water for sealing seams

Preheat oven to 350° F (180°C).

Roll dough into a rectangle. Lay ham curved side down onto dough. Gently lift dough to wrap ham securely. Be careful not to rip the dough.

Dip your fingertips in water, then rub them along seams to seal. This may take several water dips to achieve. Place ham seam side down, so it doesn't burst during baking, on a non-stick cookie sheet or shallow roasting pan. Bake 20 minutes per pound or until bread is toasty brown.

Remove ham from oven and let cool until you can touch the bread without burning your hands. With a sharp, thin knife, cut off just the top portion to create a lid. Carve the ham and remaining bread into slices. Don't worry if the bread falls apart as you slice it. This can happen. Discard any unsightly scrapes. Lay ham and bread on a serving platter. The bread will be a little soggy, and that's good, because it has soaked up the ham juices. Cover with the lid you cut off earlier.

Right before you serve, cut the lid into slices, lay them around and over the ham.

I have always had trouble cooking pork chops. They tasted good, but were tougher than the soles of my shoes. After years of failed attempts, not to mention embarrassment, I finally took matters in hand and created this recipe. This has been prepared many times for tough critics and has always been well received. Give it a try and, please, let me know how your critics respond.

Serve with Boiled Potatoes, Steamed Asparagus, and White Wine – Sauvignon Blanc.

HERB MARINATED PORK CHOPS

4 fresh sage leaves or1 tsp. (5ml) dried
3 fresh rosemary sprigs or 1 tsp. (5ml) dried
5 fresh thyme springs or 1 tsp. (5ml) dried
1 tsp. (5ml) garlic, pressed or finely chopped
1 cup (250ml) olive oil, maybe a little more
Freshly ground pepper to taste
4 pork chops with or without bones, 1 inch (2.5cm) thick
¾ cup (200ml) dry white wine
2 tbsp. (25g) butter
1 tbsp. (15ml) fresh parsley, chopped or ½ tbsp. (2.5ml) dried

Lay herbs in a glass dish large enough to hold chops in one layer. Sprinkle garlic over the herbs. Carefully pour olive oil into dish so as not to disturb herbs, then add pepper. Lay the chops across herb mixture. Add more olive oil until the chops are barely covered.

Marinate in the refrigerator 2 – 7 hours. Turn chops at least once during the time you've allowed.

Remove dish from fridge 1 hour or a little less before cooking. Meat cooks better if it's nearer room temperature.

Preheat oven to 220° F (100°C).

Add a little marinade, but not herbs, to a medium-sized frying pan and heat on medium-high until oil shimmers. Add chops and brown 3 – 4 minutes on each side until golden brown. Transfer meat to an ovenproof plate.

Pour off all but a thin film of oil, add ½ cup (120ml) wine, and bring to a boil. Return chops to pan. Cover and reduce heat to a simmer. Cook 30 minutes, basting with pan juices occasionally, until chops are tender when pierced with the tip of a sharp knife. Return meat to the ovenproof plate, cover, and set in oven while you finish the potatoes and asparagus.

Prepare sauce just before serving dinner. Skim as much fat as possible from braising liquid and pour in remaining ¼ cup (60ml) wine. Boil over high heat, stirring and scraping in any brown bits that cling to the bottom and sides of the pan, until the liquid has reduced to a syrupy glaze.

Swirl in butter and parsley off the heat. Pour sauce over pork chops and serve.

Ready for a refreshing change to a lighter menu that is wonderful any time of the year, especially in hot weather when you dine *al fresco*?

Serve with Baked Sweet Potatoes, Fresh Green Beans, and White Wine – Chardonnay.

HONEYED HAM STEAK

1 16 oz. (230g) can cling peach halves in heavy syrup
1 – 1½ lb. (450 – 900g) ham steak 1 inch (2.5cm) thick
½ cup (120ml) orange juice
1 tbsp. (15ml) honey
2 tsp. (10ml) yellow mustard
¼ tsp. (1.25ml) ground allspice
2 tbsp. (30ml) water
1 tsp. (5ml) cornstarch

Preheat oven to 220° F (100°C).

Drain peach halves, reserving ½ cup (120ml) syrup.

Trim a few pieces of fat from the ham steak. Heat a skillet over medium-high heat. Add the fat chunks and fry until lightly browned, rubbing them along the bottom of the skillet to grease it. Discard fat. Add ham and brown on both sides, 4 – 5 minutes.

Reduce heat to medium. Stir in juice, honey, mustard, allspice, and reserved peach syrup.

Add peach halves and heat through, 5 minutes. Place ham and peaches on a warm serving plate and tent with aluminum foil. Pop into oven while you finish preparing the meal.

Combine water and cornstarch in a small bowl until well blended. Stir into sauce. Cook over medium heat, stirring constantly, until mixture thickens and boils 1 – 2 minutes.

To serve, spoon sauce over ham and peaches.

Studs and I are big Chicago Bears fans and tailgate in our living room for all the games. It's a lot of fun and we share some of those games with friends who are happy to exchange recipes as we flip and sip over an open grill. The menu below works great on the stove and is fantastic on a grill!

Serve with Roasted Potatoes, Tossed Salad, Rosemary Flavored Olive Oil, and Dry White Wine – Pinot Grigio.

MARINATED PORK CHOPS BRAISED in WINE

4 pork chops, preferably with the bone
1 cup (250ml) olive oil, possibly more
1 green pepper, seeded and cut in strips
1 red pepper, seeded and cut in strips
1 onion, sliced
3 garlic cloves, pressed or chopped fine

Combine all ingredients in a glass bowl. Make sure chops are buried in the mixture. Add more oil if necessary. Cover with plastic wrap and refrigerate for two days.

Heat a frying pan on medium-high. The pan is ready when you sprinkle on water droplets and they hop around and evaporate quickly. Spoon a little oil in pan. Lay on chops and brown each side.

Lower heat to medium. Add peppers and onions. Cover pan and fry until fork tender, 20 minutes or so.

To Grill
Heat grill to medium high. Brown chops, both sides, on oiled grate.

Lower heat to medium. Move chops to a grill safe pan. Add peppers and onions. Close grill lid and fry until fork tender, 20 minutes or so.

Pork tenderloin is a meal right for any occasion. Be it a romantic evening for two with candles and soft music or a buffet dinner party, this easy menu is sure to impress.

Tenderloin comes in a plastic package that usually contains two pieces of meat. If you only use one, freeze the other to cook at a future date.

Serve with Baked Potatoes, Steamed Asparagus, and White Wine – Soave.

MARINATED PORK TENDERLOIN

1 pork tenderloin for every two people
Olive oil to cover
¼ cup (60ml) dry white wine
2 tsp. (10ml) garlic powder, not garlic salt
6 sprigs fresh parsley or 1 tsp. (5ml) dried
8 sprigs fresh thyme or 1½ tsp. (5ml) dried

Carefully cut away the silver streaks and connective tissue from the tenderloin.

Combine all ingredients in a glass bowl or plastic bag. Marinate meat in refrigerator for 2 – 6 hours.

Preheat oven to 450° F (230°C).

Remove meat from fridge 1 hour before roasting.

Discard marinade. Lay meat on a foil lined cookie sheet. Roast 20 – 30 minutes.

Let meat rest 5 – 10 minutes under a foil tent. This allows the juices to remain in the meat when sliced.

Carve tenderloin into ½ inch (1.25cm) slices and serve.

Pork chops are a favorite of Studs which meant I had to devise another recipe that was easy and tasty and this is it.

Serve with Rice, Fresh Green Beans, and White Wine – Chablis.

PORK CHOPS & APPLES

4 pork loin chops, preferably on the bone ½ inch (1.25cm) thick
2 tsp. (10ml) dried sage
Nonstick cooking spray
1 small onion, sliced and separated into rings
1 apple, cored and cut into wedges
1 cup (250ml) apple juice
2 tsp. (10ml) brown sugar
1 tbsp. (15ml) cold water
2 tsp. (10ml) cornstarch

Preheat oven to 220° F (100°C).

Trim off fat from chops. Rub sage on both sides of meat.

Coat a medium-sized frying pan with spray. Heat pan on medium until warm. Add meat, cook 5 minutes. Turn chops. Add most of the onions. Cook 5 minutes. Remove chops and onion to a plate, tent with foil, and set in oven.

Wipe pan out with a paper towel. Add remaining onion, apple wedges, juice, and sugar. Bring to a boil, reduce heat, and simmer 3 – 5 minutes until apples are crisp-tender.

Combine water and cornstarch in a cup. Pour into the skillet. Stir constantly until mixture thickens and bubbles. Continue cooking for 2 minutes, regulating heat to a slow boil.

To serve, arrange chops, rice, and green beans on dinner plates. Lay apple slices on each chop and then top with sauce.

Rice
Follow package directions, but replace half the water with chicken stock.

A meal fit for a king that takes a little time, but is well worth it. Add good conversation, some hand holding, and soft music for a special evening.

Make the stuffing a day or two ahead to free up your kitchen time.

Serve with Steamed Asparagus, Homemade Applesauce, and White Wine – Riesling.

STUFFED PORK CHOPS

3 loin chops, boneless
Stuffing, recipe found in Salads, Sauces, Sides, & Extras
1 tbsp. (15ml) olive oil
½ cup (120ml) chicken stock

Preheat oven to 325° F (160°C).

Slice a deep pocket in each chop. Pack in stuffing. Use toothpicks to hold pocket closed as much as possible.

Heat oil in a medium-sized skillet until it shimmers over medium-high heat. Add chops and brown on each side 2 – 3 minutes.

Pour stock into an ovenproof dish. Lay chops in dish. Cover tightly with aluminum foil. Bake 30 minutes.

POULTRY

Another busy day when you don't have time to spend over the stove? This tasty meal is easy and quick. The pasta is excellent on its own, but even better when partnered with chicken breasts.

Serve with Tasty Tomato Salad and White Wine – Pinot Grigio.

CHICKEN BREASTS
with SAGE BUTTERED PASTA

Chicken
3 chicken breasts, skinless and boneless
Milk
2 tbsp. (30ml) olive oil
1 clove garlic, chopped
½ tsp. (2.5ml) thyme
Freshly ground pepper to taste
½ cup (120ml) dry white wine

Lay breasts in a glass or ceramic dish, cover with milk. Let sit 3 – 9 hours. If you choose to soak more than 1 hour be sure to refrigerate. The milk adds flavor and also tenderizes the meat. I learned this from a very talented chef in Austria.

Preheat oven to 220° F (100°C).

Heat oil in a skillet set over medium heat. Pat breasts dry. Add them to the pan along with the garlic. Sprinkle on thyme and pepper. Sauté 15 – 20 minutes until juices run clear. Be careful not to overdo or the breasts will be dry.

Move chicken to a plate, cover with foil, and set in the oven while you deglaze the pan.

Turn temperature to medium-high. Carefully pour in wine. Stir in any browned bits that cling to the sides and bottom of the pan. Reduce this sauce by at least one-third.

Drizzle sauce over the breasts when you're ready to serve.

Pasta
8 tbsp. (1 stick) (113.5g) butter, room temperature
6 – 10 sage leaves, fresh or dried
2 cups (280g) curly pasta
Parmesan cheese, grated

Cook pasta according to package directions. Set aside while you make the sauce.

Melt butter in a frying pan over medium heat.

Add sage. Allow butter to brown. Watch carefully and stir often as once this starts to brown it can quickly burn. Cook until butter reaches a medium caramel color. Remove sage leaves and discard.

Stir in pasta. Be sure to coat the noodles well. Heat through and then serve with plenty of Parmesan cheese.

This is a lovely meal for two to share by candlelight or with family and friends and rousing conversation. It's also perfect *al fresco* on a Sunday afternoon.

Serve with Roasted Potatoes, Candied Orange Carrots, and White Wine – Chardonnay.

CHICKEN CUTLETS

5 slices bacon, chopped
¼ (30g) cup flour
3 chicken breasts, skinless and boneless
1 tbsp. (15ml) butter
4 garlic cloves, pressed or chopped fine
1 tbsp. (15ml) fresh rosemary, chopped or 1 tsp. dried
¼ tsp. (1.25ml) red pepper flakes
1 cup (250ml) chicken stock
2 tbsp. (30ml) lemon juice
Freshly ground pepper to taste

Fry bacon over medium heat until crisp. Transfer bacon onto paper towels to drain. Spoon off all but two tablespoons (30ml) of fat.

Meanwhile, place flour in a shallow dish. Dredge chicken in flour and shake to remove excess. Add butter to reserved fat in pan and heat over medium-high temperature, swirling to melt butter. When the foam subsides, reduce heat to medium and cook chicken until browned on both sides, 4 – 6 minutes per side. Transfer chicken to a plate and tent with foil.

Stir in garlic, rosemary, pepper flakes. Cook 45 – 60 seconds. Do not let the garlic brown. Add stock and lemon juice. Scrape browned bits clinging to the bottom and sides into the sauce. Simmer until slightly thickened, 4 minutes.

Return chicken and bacon to pan. Simmer, turning chicken once, until sauce is thick and glossy, 2 – 3 minutes. Adjust seasoning with pepper.

Slice breasts into wide strips as pictured for a more dramatic presentation right before you serve. Be sure to drizzle sauce over the pieces.

Time for a little Southern style comfort food. This meal is tasty and also easy because it's a one pot event. An added bonus is that it freezes great.

Serve with Tossed Salad and White Wine – Riesling.

CHICKEN & DUMPLINGS

1 qt. (1L) chicken stock
2 carrots, scraped and diced
Freshly ground pepper to taste
1 lb. (450g) cooked chicken breasts and/or thighs, skinned and boned*
1 tbsp. (15ml) cold water
2 tsp. (10ml) cornstarch
Dried parsley for garnish

Chicken

Pour stock into a 5 quart (1.5L) saucepan. You need that size so the dumplings cook properly and you have leftover stew and dumplings to freeze. Add carrots and pepper. Bring to a boil. Lower heat and simmer 20 minutes.

Tear or cut meat into bite size pieces. Add to pan.

Combine water and cornstarch, then stir into saucepan.

*It's no problem if you don't have cooked chicken on hand. Simply place your fresh or thawed chicken pieces in the same pot you'll use for the meal with 1 quart water. Bring to a boil then lower the heat and simmer for 45 minutes. Remove chicken and let cool before you tear it. Pour cooking water into a bowl to cool. Skim off as much fat as possible then pour into containers and freeze for future use when you boil potatoes or steam vegetables.

Dumplings

Yes, I cheat by using a box mix. I freely admit it and I'm not ashamed. Well, maybe a little.

2 cups (350g) dumpling mix – I prefer Bisquick®

⅔ cup (150ml) milk

Combine mix and milk in a bowl. Mix until a soft dough forms.

Return chicken and stock to a boil. Drop dough by large spoonfuls onto stock. It doesn't matter if the dumplings clump together.

Reduce heat to simmer. Cook uncovered for 10 minutes. Cover the pot and cook another 10 minutes.

To serve, ladle into soup bowls then sprinkle with dried parsley for color.

Leftovers freeze well for up to 2 months.

If time constraints demand a tasty and fast dinner then this is the meal for you. Should you prefer a slower paced evening with a little romance, this is still the meal for you. Light a few candles and turn on the soft music and let the mood sweep you away.

Serve with Rice, Tossed Salad, and White Wine – Rhine.

CHICKEN STIR-FRY

1½ lb. (750g) chicken thighs, skinless, boneless, and cut into strips
½ tsp. (2.5ml) ground ginger
Freshly ground pepper to taste
2 tbsp. (30ml) vegetable oil
Splash sesame seed or olive oil
½ red pepper, cleaned and cut into strips
1 small head broccoli, trimmed into florets
10 baby carrots, cut in half lengthwise
10 mini bella mushrooms, cut in half lengthwise
1 small onion, halved and sliced
2 garlic cloves, sliced
¾ cup (60ml) chicken stock
1 tbsp. (45ml) soy sauce
2 tbsp. (30ml) cornstarch

Combine chicken, ginger, and pepper in glass or ceramic bowl. Set aside.

On medium-high heat, warm oil in wok or large frying pan until it shimmers. Fry chicken until no longer pink, 3 – 5 minutes. Remove from pan to a clean bowl.

Add vegetables and garlic to pan and stir-fry to crisp tender, 4 – 6 minutes.

Stir stock, soy sauce, and cornstarch in a small bowl until well blended. Scrape into hot skillet. Add chicken and pepper. Cook over high heat, stirring constantly, until mixture thickens and bubbles.

Here's a dish to make your mouth water and it won't break the bank. Leftovers don't freeze well, but the dish does last up to two days in the refrigerator and nukes beautifully.

Serve with Pasta, Caesar Salad, and Red Wine – Chianti.

Yes, I know this is chicken, but a good Chianti really sets off the meal.

CHICKEN THIGHS with an ITALIAN FLAIR

4 chicken thighs, skinless and boneless
4 slices prosciutto
1 tsp. (5ml) marjoram
½ cup (60g) flour
2 tbsp. (30ml) olive oil
1 12 – 14 oz. (352 - 410g) can tomato sauce
½ cup (120ml) dry white wine
2 tbsp. (30ml) fresh basil, chopped, or 1 tbsp. (15ml) dried
Freshly grated Parmesan cheese

Gently pound thighs slightly thinner between two pieces of waxed paper. Remove wax paper. Sprinkle lightly with marjoram. Lay prosciutto onto thighs, replace wax paper, and gently pound.

Pour flour into a paper bag. Place one thigh at a time inside bag and shake gently. Remove thigh to a plate while you flour the remaining thighs.

Heat olive oil in a large skillet over medium-high heat until it shimmers. Carefully add thighs chicken side down. Fry until nicely browned. Turn meat. Regulate heat so chicken browns and doesn't burn.

Pour tomato sauce over chicken. Add wine, basil, and gently stir. Cover and simmer 10 – 12 minutes. Sprinkle a good amount of cheese across the top. Heat through.

To serve, place chicken on a plate along with your favorite pasta. Ladle pan juices over the pasta. Be sure to have a bowl of grated cheese on the table.

You may want to increase the ingredient amounts for this delectable dish since it freezes well.

Serve with Baked Sweet Potato, Steamed Asparagus, Cherry Tomatoes and White Wine – Chardonnay.

EASY BAKED CHICKEN BREAST

Non-stick cooking spray
3 chicken breasts, boneless and skinless
½ cup (60g) mayonnaise
5 tsp. (25ml) Italian seasoned dry bread crumbs
½ cup (60g) Parmesan cheese, grated

Preheat oven to 425° F (220°C).

Spray a baking dish lightly with cooking spray. Rinse chicken and pat dry.

Mix mayo and bread crumbs together in a small bowl. Spread onto both sides of chicken.

Lay chicken in prepared dish. Sprinkle the top of coated chicken with Parmesan cheese.

Bake for 20 minutes or until the juices run clear when chicken is pierced with a sharp knife.

Studs and I have served this meal many times to family and friends and they're always surprised to learn it's actually Italian. Keep this recipe handy. It's perfect when you dine *al fresco* on a summer evening.

Serve with Curly Pasta, Salad with Creamy Garlic Dressing, and White Wine – Soave.

MUSTARD CHICKEN with CURLY PASTA

5 chicken thighs, skinless and boneless
8 tbsp. (1 stick) (113.5g) butter, melted
¼ cup (30g) Dijon mustard
4 tbsp. (60ml) lemon or lime juice
2 rounded tbsp. (30g) brown sugar
Freshly ground pepper to taste
2 tsp. (10ml) paprika
3 tbsp. (45ml) poppy seeds, optional
Freshly grated Parmesan cheese

Preheat oven to 400° F (200°C).

Lay chicken into an ovenproof dish.

Combine all ingredients, except poppy seeds and pasta, in a small bowl. Coat chicken evenly with half the mixture. Bake 15 minutes.

Remove dish from oven and carefully turn chicken over. Spread remaining sauce over the pieces. Sprinkle on poppy seeds. Return to oven and bake 15 minutes.

Pasta
1 lb. campanelle pasta, shells, or other curly pasta

Cook per package directions. Be sure to cook al dente, no more.

Arrange the Dish

Ladle drained pasta into a serving dish. Add some of the juice from the cooked chicken pan and stir. Lay chicken across the pasta. Pour the remaining sauce over the top.

Add a bowl of freshly grated Parmesan cheese to the table to sprinkle on the chicken and pasta.

Leftovers freeze well.

Dress dinner up with candles, soft music, and wine for a lovely two people evening. But if your time is short, there's no reason not to still enjoy this meal.

**Serve with Rice, Caesar Salad, and
White Wine – Sauvignon Blanc.**

SAUTÉED CHICKEN BREAST

3 chicken breasts, boneless and skinless
Milk
2 tbsp. (30ml) olive oil
Chicken stock fresh or canned as needed
1 tbsp. (15ml) dried marjoram
3 tbsp. (45ml) fresh parsley, chopped or 1½ tbsp. (20ml) dried

Place the breasts in a glass dish, cover with milk, and let sit for a minimum of 3 hours. You can also soak them overnight. If you choose to soak for more than 3 hours be sure to refrigerate the dish. I learned this from a very talented chef in Salzburg, Austria.

Preheat oven to 220° F (100°C).

Set your dishes or platter in the oven to warm.

Pat chicken dry. Sprinkle marjoram over the meat evenly. Heat oil in a skillet set over medium heat. Sauté breasts until the juices run clear 20 – 25 minutes. Be careful not to overcook. Should the chicken look dry at any point add a bit of stock.

To serve, spoon rice onto the warmed plates or platter. Lay breasts on top. Sprinkle with parsley and serve.

Any time is down-home cooking time. So tie your apron on and let's get to it! Forget the wine. It does not go well with this dinner.

Serve with Mashed Potatoes, Fresh Green Beans, and Your Favorite Beverage.

SLOANE'S FRIED CHICKEN

1 tbsp. (15ml) salt
Tap water
6 chicken legs or thighs or 4 skinless and boneless breasts
1 cup (100g) flour
1tsp. (5ml) thyme
½ tsp. (2.5ml) marjoram
Freshly ground pepper to taste
1 large egg
1½ tbsp. (20ml) milk
½ cup (60g) solid shortening or lard, plus more as needed

Dissolve salt in a small amount of water. Add chicken pieces then cover with more water. Set in the refrigerator 4 – 8 hours.

Remove chicken from fridge 2 hours before you plan to cook it. When you're ready, drain chicken and pat dry.

Combine flour and seasonings in a paper or plastic bag. Shake gently to combine ingredients. Mix egg and milk in a bowl. Set a platter on the counter to hold the breaded chicken in one layer.

Place one chicken piece at a time in bag, shake gently to thoroughly coat, then dip in egg mixture, then return the piece to the bag and gently shake again. Set chicken on plate. Repeat process until all pieces are coated. Place the uncovered plate in fridge for at least 30 minutes. This allows the coating to dry and cling better to the chicken as you fry it.

Heat shortening in a large frying pan set over medium-high heat. Test to be sure shortening is hot enough by adding a small piece of bread. It should sizzle and toast quickly.

Carefully add chicken pieces. Maintain temperature, but adjust it so chicken doesn't burn and grease doesn't splatter everywhere.

Turn frequently to brown chicken on all sides. Lower temperature to medium. Cover and cook 20 minutes or until juices run clear when pierced with the tip of a sharp knife. Another way to tell is meat will pull away from leg and thigh bones when the chicken is cooked. Be sure not to overcook or the meat will be dry.

Lay pieces on a plate lined with paper towels to absorb any oil. Transfer them to a clean platter and serve.

Leftover breasts make great chicken sandwiches the next day.

FISH & SEAFOOD

Baked salmon steaks are a delightful treat and not outrageously expensive. Tease your taste buds with this combination of sweet and spicy.

**Serve with Rice, Steamed Asparagus, and
White Wine – Pinot Grigio.**

BAKED SALMON

Non-stick cooking spray
3 salmon fillets, no more than 1 inch (2.5cm) thick
¼ cup (30g) brown sugar
¼ cup (30g) Dijon mustard
½ tbsp. (10ml) white wine
2 tbsp. (30ml) butter
1 tbsp. (15ml) pine nuts
3 scallions/green onions, sliced, be sure to include much of the green

Preheat oven to 425° F (220°C).

Spray aluminum foil and lay it on a cookie sheet. Place fish on foil.

Combine sugar, mustard, and wine in a small bowl. Whisk until smooth.

Spread mixture evenly over salmon to cover it. Bake 15 minutes or until fish flakes with a fork.

Meanwhile, prepare green onion topping while salmon bakes. Melt butter in a small frying pan. Add nuts, they give the dish extra crunch. Stir in onion. Sauté until onion is soft and lightly colored. Set aside.

Turn oven to broil. Move fish to 4 inches from heat. Broil 2 minutes or until golden.

Add a dollop of green onion mixture on top of each salmon steak and serve.

My longtime friend Bonnie adapted the following recipe from her longtime friend Sharon. Of course, I had to make a few changes of my own. No matter if you use all the ingredients or just some. We three cooks agree this fish is wonderful!

Serve with Baked Sweet Potatoes, Tomato & Cucumber Salad, and White Wine – Rhine.

BAKED WALLEYE

2 tbsp. (30ml) butter
3 scallions/green onions, chopped include most of the green
8 – 10 mini bella mushrooms, sliced
1 – 1½ lbs. (½ – 1kg) walleye fillets, skinless
Freshly ground pepper to taste
1 tsp. (5ml) marjoram
½ tsp. (2.5ml) garlic powder, not garlic salt
2 tbsp. (30ml) dry white wine
2 tsp. (10ml) lemon juice
1 handful cheddar cheese, shredded
⅓ cup (37g) Parmesan cheese, grated
1 handful seasoned breadcrumbs
½ cup (114g) butter, melted
2 tbsp. (30ml) fresh parsley, chopped or 1 tbsp. (5ml) dried

Preheat oven to 400° F (200°C).

Butter an ovenproof dish that holds the fish in one level. A 9 x 13 inch (23 x 33cm) glass dish works great. Scatter onions over the bottom, top with mushrooms. Lay fish over veggies.

Season the dish with pepper, marjoram, and garlic. Sprinkle on wine and lemon juice.

Spread cheeses and breadcrumbs evenly across the dish. Drizzle on butter.

Bake 7 minutes then cover with foil. Bake 4 minutes longer or until fish flakes easily with a fork.

Serve on warmed individual plates with a sprinkle of parsley across the top.

There are days Studs and I want a change of pace weekend lunch. This menu is made up with the perfect foods. It's best to make the tartar sauce and fries before you start the fish.

Serve with Homemade Fries, Tartar Sauce, and cold beer or soda.

FRESH FISH SANDWICH

2 tsp. (10ml) olive oil, plus more for brushing
2 fresh deli rolls, split
2 slices provolone cheese
2 basa or swai fillets or any other mild white fish
1 clove garlic, pressed or chopped fine
4 sage leaves or ½ tsp. (2.5ml) dried
3 thyme sprigs or ½ tsp. (2.5ml) dried
1 tsp. (5ml) parsley
Freshly ground pepper to taste
Tartar sauce to taste
Lettuce, tomato, and onion, optional

Heat skillet or grill pan over medium-high heat. Brush a little olive oil onto insides of the rolls. Test skillet for heat by sprinkling a few drops of water onto the pan. When the water jumps and quickly evaporates place rolls, oiled side down, onto cooking surface. Carefully toast until the rolls are a light golden brown. Remove to individual plates and lay a slice of cheese on bottom half.

Pour remaining olive oil into hot skillet. When the oil shimmers add fish. Sprinkle with herbs. Fry 2-3 minutes per side or until fish flakes easily with a fork. Thicker fillets require a longer cook time so be patient if you opt for cod.

Remove fish from skillet with a spatula and lay fillets on cheese half of the rolls. Add a healthy smear of tartar sauce, the lettuce and tomato, then cap with the other half of the roll and enjoy.

Quick and easy and oh so tasty, this recipe is sure to become one of your favorites.

**Serve with Baked Potatoes, Fresh Green Beans,
and White Wine – Moselle.**

LIME INFUSED SOLE

¼ cup (30g) flour
3 sole fillets or any mild white fish
4 tbsp. (57g) butter
2 limes, ends trimmed and sliced into thin circles
2 tbsp. (30ml) capers, drained

Pour flour into a paper or plastic bag. Add one fillet and gently shake the bag to coat fish. Shake to remove excess flour and set fillet on a plate. Do the same with the remaining fillets.

Melt 1 tablespoon (15g) butter in a large skillet over medium-high heat. Add limes and cook until they are lightly browned, 2 – 4 minutes. Push limes off to the side.

Add 1 tablespoon (15g) butter and the fish. Fry until the sole flakes easily, 2 – 4 minutes per side.

Add remaining butter and capers. Remove skillet from heat and tilt pan to swirl butter until it melts.

Transfer fish and limes to warmed individual plates. Spoon sauce over the top and serve immediately.

I was inspired to create this menu after Studs and I enjoyed a fun-filled long weekend in Memphis, Tennessee. Now that's a city with great music and amazing food. Be sure to prepare the sides and sauce before you start the fish.

Serve with Homemade Fries, Snazzy Sliced Tomatoes, Remoulade Sauce, and Cold Beer.

PAN-FRIED CATFISH FILLETS

⅓ cup (40g) all-purpose flour, might need a little more
½ tsp. (2.5ml) freshly ground pepper
2 tbsp. (30ml) water
2 eggs, beaten
½ cup (60g) seasoned breadcrumbs
¼ cup (30g) cornmeal
¼ tsp. (1.25ml) red pepper flakes
⅛ tsp. (.60ml) garlic powder
½ tsp. (2.5ml) dried sage
½ tsp. (2.5ml) dried thyme
4 catfish fillets, cut into serving pieces
2 tbsp. (25g) lard, solid shortening, or vegetable oil
1 tbsp. (15g) butter

Combine flour and pepper in a plastic or paper bag. Mix water and eggs in a shallow dish large enough to hold a fillet. Blend breadcrumbs, cornmeal, and remaining dry ingredients in a second shallow dish.

Place one fish in the bag and shake gently to coat. Remove and dip in egg mixture. Dredge in breadcrumbs mixture. Lay on a plate. Do the same with the other pieces. Do not stack or overlap the fish. Set in the refrigerator 20 – 30 minutes. This dries the breading a little and helps it adhere better while frying.

Heat a large nonstick skillet over medium heat. Add oil and butter to pan. Swirl pan to melt butter. Be careful not to burn it. Add fillets to pan. Cook 5 minutes on each side or until fish flakes easily with a fork.

Here's a quick and easy meal sure to impress your special someone.

Serve with Orzo or Curly Pasta, Leafy Greens with Creamy Garlic Dressing, and White Wine – Soave.

SAUTÉED SEA SCALLOPS

1 ½ lb. (750g) sea scallops
1 ½ tbsp. (20ml) olive oil
2 tbsp. (30ml) butter
2 tsp. (10ml) garlic, chopped
Freshly ground pepper to taste
½ cup (120ml) dry white wine
1 tsp. (5ml) chives, snipped for garnish

Preheat oven to 220° F (100°C).

Rinse and pat dry the scallops.

Combine olive oil and butter in a frying pan set on medium-high heat. Add scallops when the foam subsides. Sear 2 – 4 minutes per side. Make sure they are golden edging into brown before you turn them.

Add garlic when you turn the scallops.

After scallops reach the proper color, remove them to a bowl. Set in oven to keep warm while you prepare the sauce.

Spoon out garlic from the frying pan. Skim off some of the fat that has floated to the top. Carefully add the wine, all the while scraping in any browned pieces that cling to the sides and bottom of the pan. Cook until the mixture reduces by a third.

Lay scallops on a bed of orzo either on a platter or individual plates. Lace the sauce over the dish. Top with chives and serve.

Sloane Taylor

This delicious dinner is a breeze to prepare. It's the perfect meal for busy schedules when you only have a short time to share with your partner.

Serve with Baked Potatoes, Sautéed Broccoli, and White Wine – Chablis.

SEARED TILAPIA

¼ cup (30g) flour
3 tilapia fillets or any mild white fish
4 tbsp. (57g) butter
Splash or 2 of white wine
1 tsp. (5ml) chives, snipped
1 tbsp. (15ml) lemon juice
Freshly ground pepper to taste

Pour flour into a paper or plastic bag. Add one fillet and gently shake bag to coat fish. Remove fillet and wiggle it to eliminate excess flour. Set fillet on a plate. Do the same with the remaining fish.

Melt 2 tablespoons (25g) butter in a large skillet over medium-high heat. Add wine and fish. Fry until the tilapia flakes easily with a fork, 2 – 4 minutes per side.

Add remaining butter, chives, and lemon juice. Remove skillet from heat and tilt the pan to swirl the butter until it melts. Add pepper.

Transfer fish to individual plates. Spoon the sauce over the top.

60

You'll be pleasantly surprised by the enticing aroma from this easy recipe and the taste is superb. Studs and I have served this menu to skeptical guests and they fell in love with it.

Cook pasta before you start fish. Re-warm by pouring hot water over the noodles before serving.

Serve with Whole Grain Spaghetti, Tossed Salad, Italian Bread, and White Wine – Pinot Grigio.

TANTALIZING COD

1 tbsp. (15ml) olive oil
½ medium onion, sliced thin
2 garlic cloves, pressed or chopped fine
½ cup (120ml) dry white wine
5 large Roma tomatoes, chopped
½ cup (60g) black olives, sliced
2 tbsp. (30ml) fresh parsley, chopped or 1 tbsp. (15g) dried
1 tbsp. (15ml) capers, drained and chopped
¼ tsp. (1.25ml) crushed red pepper
4 cod fillets about 6 oz.(190g) each
½ tbsp. (8ml) fresh basil, chopped or 1 tsp. (5ml) dried

Heat a large skillet on medium-high. Add oil. Heat until it shimmers. Add onion, stir until translucent and lightly colored. Stir in garlic, cook 30 seconds. Add wine, cook 1 minute. Stir in tomatoes with the juice, olives, parsley, capers, and red pepper. Heat to boiling.

Lay cod fillets over tomato mixture. Lower heat to medium. Cover skillet and cook until cod turns opaque throughout and flakes, 9 minutes.

Sprinkle basil across the top.

Serve over whole grain spaghetti.

Don't prepare extra. Leftovers have a stale taste and tend to be tough.

Studs and I enjoy making this meal together. He does the salad while I cook the fish and rice. Of course we sip a little wine while working.

Serve with Rice, Tossed Salad, and White Wine – Riesling.

TILAPIA with a CITRUS TWIST

1½ tbsp. (21g) butter
1 tbsp. (15ml) extra virgin olive oil plus 1 tsp. (5ml)
½ tsp. (2.5ml) anchovy paste
2 cloves garlic, pressed
1 tbsp. (15ml) orange juice plus ½ tsp (2.5ml).
½ tsp. (2.5ml) lemon juice
3 tilapia filets
1 tbsp. (15ml) fresh basil, chopped or 1 tsp. (5ml) dried
Freshly ground pepper to taste

Sauce
Add butter and olive oil to a small pan set on medium heat. Stir in anchovy paste until it dissolves. Add garlic, cook until fragrant, 30 seconds. Remove from heat. Stir in orange and lemon juices. Keep warm over low heat.

Sauce can be made 1 day ahead. If you do then cool, cover, and refrigerate. Warm before using.

Fish
Brush remaining olive oil over fish. Sprinkle fish with basil and pepper. Heat a pan over medium heat. Add tilapia and fry until opaque and flakes easily with a fork, 3 minutes per side. Drizzle sauce over fish and serve.

INTERNATIONAL DISHES

No International section of a cookbook is complete without a traditional dish from Russia. Especially one that is easy and satisfying. This hearty recipe serves two with wonderful leftovers. Simply increase the ingredient amounts proportionally to serve a larger group.

Serve with Egg Noodles, Tossed Salad, and Red Wine – Pinot Noir.

BEEF STROGANOFF

ГОВЯДИНА БЕФСТРОГАНОВ

4 oz. (125g) sour cream, reduced fat works well
2 tbsp. (30ml) tomato paste
1 tsp. (5ml) Worcestershire sauce
¼ cup (30g) flour
Freshly ground pepper to taste
1 lb. (500g) good steak like porterhouse, t-bone, or sirloin
1 tbsp. (15ml) olive oil
½ cup (60g) onion, thinly sliced

1 cup (250ml) beef stock, maybe a bit more to achieve the consistency you prefer
1 cup (100g) mushrooms, sliced but not too thin
Fresh parsley, chopped
¼ pkg. egg noodles

Combine sour cream, tomato paste, and Worcestershire sauce in a small bowl. Set aside while you prepare the remainder of the recipe.

Trim off fat and cut steak into narrow strips. Combine flour and pepper in a paper or plastic bag. Add steak pieces, a few at a time, and gently shake to coat the meat. Set pieces on a plate as you coat them.

Melt butter and oil in a large frying pan. Add onions and sauté for 3 – 5 minutes. You want the onions soft but not browned. Add beef, turn up heat to medium-high. Sauté meat until browned, turn often so it doesn't burn, 5 – 7 minutes. Slowly pour in stock, scraping pan to combine browned bits into the mixture. Reduce heat to medium. Stir in mushrooms, cover, and cook until meat is tender, 3 – 5 minutes. Reduce heat to low. Stir in sour cream mixture by heaping spoonfuls. If the sauce looks too thick, slowly add a bit more beef stock until you achieve the consistency you prefer. Cook uncovered 1 – 3 minutes or until hot. Do NOT let pan come to a boil.

Egg Noodles
Follow the package directions to cook. If the noodles are done before the Stroganoff, drain them in a colander and set the pot or lid on top of the noodles to keep them warm.

REMEMBER: all noodles/pasta can easily be re-warmed by pouring hot water over them before serving.

To serve, scoop egg noodles into soup/salad bowls. Spoon hearty portions of Stroganoff over the noodles and then scatter on parsley.

Leftovers are excellent. Refrigerate noodles and meat in separate containers. To reheat the Stroganoff pour it into a saucepan, add a little beef stock to thin it, and warm through. The noodles are easy as well to reheat. Bring a small pan of water to a boil. Add the noodles for a few seconds then drain.

This dish from Italy may seem like a lot of work, but it really isn't. You will love the beautiful blend of flavors. The recipe serves two, maybe three. Double it and freeze the extra for another meal.

Serve with Caesar Salad and White Wine – Soave.

CHICKEN CASSEROLE

POLLO TETRAZZINI

Chicken
2 chicken breasts, skinless and boneless
1 medium onion, peeled and halved
1 whole clove
1 stalk celery, including leaves, chopped
1 bay leaf
1 medium carrot, chopped
5 cups (1¼L) chicken stock

Combine chicken and all remaining ingredients in a medium-sized saucepan. Bring to a boil over high heat. Reduce temperature to low and simmer, partially covered for 15 – 25 minutes, or until chicken is tender but not falling apart.

Transfer chicken to a cutting board. When cool enough to handle, cut chicken into 1 inch pieces. Set aside.

Strain cooking liquid through a fine sieve set over a bowl. Press down hard on the vegetables with the back of a spoon before you discard them. Skim the grease that rises to the top. Reserve the stock to use later in this recipe.

Noodles
½ lb. (230g) broad egg noodles

Cook noodles per package directions but only for 6 minutes. They will cook more when you bake the casserole. Drain noodles in a colander and rinse under cold water. Set aside.

Mushrooms
6 tbsp. (85g) butter
8 oz. (250g) mini bella mushrooms, sliced

Melt butter in a small skillet set on moderate heat. Stir in mushrooms and cook 5 minutes, or until barely tender. Set aside.

Sauce
6 tbsp. (85g) butter
6 tbsp. (85g) flour
½ cup (120ml) heavy cream
½ cup (120ml) dry sherry
2 egg yolks
½ tsp. (2.5ml) hot sauce
Parsley for garnish

Melt butter in a medium-sized saucepan set on medium heat. Whisk in flour and mix thoroughly. Gradually add 2 cups (500ml) of reserved stock, cream, and sherry. Cook over high heat until this blend comes to a boil. Reduce heat to low.

Whisk yolks in a small bowl. Slowly add ½ cup (120ml) of hot liquid while whisking constantly. Now reverse the process and stir egg mixture into the saucepan. Cook 1 – 2 minutes, then stir in hot sauce. Remove pan from heat.

To Assemble and Bake
2 tbsp. (25g) butter, softened
1 cup (113g) Parmesan cheese, grated

Preheat oven to 350° F (180°C).

Coat the bottom and sides of an 8 x 10 inch (20 x 25cm) baking dish, or a dish as close as you have, with butter. Pour in 1 cup (250ml) of sauce and scatter half the noodles over the bottom. Spread on half the mushrooms, and then cover with half the chicken. Repeat layers and top with remaining sauce. Sprinkle cheese over the dish.

Bake 30 minutes.

Sprinkle fresh or dried parsley across the dish before you serve.

This recipe freezes beautifully. Thaw and add a little cream to the leftovers. Bake for 15 – 25 minutes at 325° F (160°C).

Here is an Americanized version of an ancient Chinese dish. Grab your chopsticks and dig right in.

But I must say it gripes me to no end to see chop suey meat in the grocery store hovering close to $5.00 a pound. Those fatty chunks are scraps the butcher carved off who knows what, or when, and lumped into a package for us consumers to blithely purchase.

Don't do it!

Over the years, I have learned it is best, and cheaper, to buy small beef and pork roasts on sale. At least I know what meat I'm actually using in my recipes. The unused portion of the roasts are easily frozen for future recipes.

**Serve with Egg Rolls, Rice, Hot Tea,
and White Wine – Saki or Chardonnay.**

CHOP SUEY WITH A KICK

2 lbs. (1kg) boneless beef roast, trimmed of fat and connective tissue
1 lb. (500g) boneless pork roast, trimmed of fat and connective tissue
2 tbsp. (30ml) olive oil, you may need a little more
2 tbsp. (25g) butter
3 celery ribs, chopped
1 cup (100g) onion, chopped
2 cups (450ml) beef stock
4 tbsp. (60ml) cornstarch
2 tbsp. (30ml) bead molasses
3 tbsp. (45ml) soya sauce
1 can bean sprouts, drained
1 can sliced water chestnuts, drained
1 tsp. (5ml) crushed red pepper – the more you add, the bigger the kick
1 clove garlic, pressed or chopped fine

Fresh mushrooms, sliced thick - optional
Freshly ground pepper to taste

Cut the meats into 2 inch (5cm) cubes.

Over medium-high heat, combine oil and butter in a large pot. When foam subsides, brown the meat in batches. Be sure not to overcrowd the pot. When the batch is browned, remove to a bowl. Continue until all meat is browned.

Add celery and onions, sauté until soft, 5 – 7 minutes.

Lower heat to medium. Return meat to pot. Blend beef stock and cornstarch, then stir into pot. Add bead molasses and soya sauce. Stir well.

Mix in bean sprouts, water chestnuts, red pepper, and garlic. Cover pot and simmer 1 hour.

Add mushrooms and black pepper 10 minutes before chop suey is finished.

Serve over rice. Chop suey freezes well for future meals.

Rice
Your favorite brand
Chicken stock

Prepare rice following package directions, but exchange half the water with chicken stock.

Egg Rolls
Many grocery stores sell egg rolls in the deli section. If you go this route, reheat them at 350° F (180°C) for 15 – 20 minutes.

The other day my store was out so I used Tai Pei Mini Vegetable Spring Rolls, found in the freezer section. The bag holds 15 rolls and 2 sauce packets. No MSG is added and they have zero trans fat. They baked up crisp in 12 minutes at 450° F (230°C). The taste and texture were wonderful!

Serve egg rolls as an appetizer just before the rest of your meal is done cooking.

I like to mix up our meals with foods from different countries. Not only does that add variety, but sparks dinnertime conversation. This menu is a traditional Polish meal, updated by Studs, farmers and hill people have enjoyed for centuries. You know, sometimes peasant food really is the best.

Serve with Boiled Potatoes, Sauerkraut, Mizeria, Polish Style Cucumbers, Bakery Rye Bread, Cold Beer, and don't forget the Horseradish.

POLISH SAUSAGE

KIELBASA

4 lbs. (2kg) fresh Polish sausage links*
Tap water

Remove sausage from refrigerator at least 1 hour before cooking.

Fill a stockpot approximately ¾ with cold tap water. Bring to a boil over high heat.

Add sausage and cook 10 minutes once the water starts to boil. The sausage should rise to the top in 5 minutes. Transfer links to shallow roasting pans. Clip the connecting casing.

You can stop here and finish cooking the sausage the next day. Be sure to cover and refrigerate the meat.

Preheat oven to 325° F (160°C).

Bake for 15 minutes. Remove pan from oven. Turn sausage pieces and then bake another 15 minutes.

Allow sausage to rest 10 – 15 minutes so the juices are reabsorbed into the meat.

Cut the links into 1½ - 2 inch (4 – 5cm) pieces.

Not a problem if you have leftover sausage. The meat stays good five days in the fridge and freezes well for future meals. Simply thaw, cover, and reheat in the oven for 20 minutes at 325° F (160°C).

*When shopping, calculate ¾ pound (375g) raw sausage per person.

How about a quick trip to Austria for a delicious dish that is *uber* easy to prepare?

Weiner Schnitzel was created by a chef in Vienna around 1845. The recipe called for veal and the government passed a law, still in effect, that it was illegal to sell Weiner Schnitzel made with anything but veal.

Economical cooks in Austria and Germany were not daunted. They let their creativity soar and so did I in this version of Pork Schnitzel.

Serve with Boiled Potatoes or Spätzle, White Asparagus or Brussels Sprouts, Homemade Applesauce, and White Wine – Lebfraumilch.

PORK CUTLET

SCHWEINESCHNITZEL

2 boneless pork loin chops

½ cup (60g) all-purpose flour
Freshly ground pepper to taste
1 large egg
¼ cup (60ml) milk
1 cup (100g) Panko bread crumbs
¼ cup (52g or 60ml) lard or olive oil
2 tbsp. (30ml) butter
2 sprigs fresh thyme or ¼ tsp. (1.25ml) dried
2 tbsp. (25g) lard, solid shortening, or vegetable oil
Lemon slices, optional

Place each chop between 2 sheets of plastic wrap or wax paper. Use a mallet or the side of a meat tenderizer to gently pound them until they are ¼ inch (.5cm) thick. Make several small cuts along the edges so the meat doesn't curl as it fries.

Combine flour and pepper in a shallow dish or paper bag. Whisk egg and milk together in another dish. Pour Panko into a third dish.

Dredge chops in flour, then egg mixture, and finally Panko. Press the breadcrumbs onto the pork so there is an even coating.

Lay the breaded pork on a plate lined with parchment or waxed paper. Set in refrigerator uncovered for a half hour. This dries the coating and allows it to adhere better during cooking.

Add lard or oil and butter to a large skillet set over medium heat.

If using fresh thyme, add the sprigs and fry for 2 minutes to infuse the oil. Remove thyme and discard.

If you use dried thyme, sprinkle it on the pork before adding to the pan.

Lay meat into pan and cook until golden brown and crispy, 3 – 5 minutes per side. Adjust heat as needed so as not to burn the coating.

Set cooked meat on a paper towel lined plate to absorb any excess oil.

Garnish with lemon slices, if desired, and serve immediately.

France – the country where Can Can was a scandalous dance in the days of Toulouse-Lautrec and *Haute cuisine* reigned. And it still does. Be it a Michelin-starred restaurant or a rural farm house, quality and presentation are most important. This dinner fits comfortably in that elite category without a lot of work. So grab your partner, tie-on your apron, and create a dinner of sheer bliss.

Serve with Parsley Potatoes, Snow Peas with Lettuce, and Red Wine – Cabernet Sauvignon.

SAUTÉED STEAK with RED WINE SAUCE

BIFTECK MARCHAND DE VINS

Sauce
1 tbsp. (15ml) butter
¼ cup (30g) scallions/green onions, chopped fine, be sure to include the green part
¾ cup (60ml) dry red wine
1 small bay leaf

¼ tsp. (1.25ml) dried thyme
4 parsley sprigs or ½ tsp. (2.5ml) dried
¼ cup (60ml) beef stock
6 tbsp. (85g) butter, softened
½ tbsp. (7.5ml) lemon juice
½ tsp. (2.5ml) flour
½ tbsp. (7.5ml) parsley, chopped fine or 1 tsp. (5ml) dried

Melt 1 tablespoon (15ml) butter over medium heat in a small saucepan. Stir in the onions when the foam subsides. Cook 2 minutes, stirring constantly, or until they are soft but not brown. Pour in wine, add the three herbs. Simmer over moderate heat until this has reduced to ⅓ cup (75ml), 10 – 15 minutes.

Strain the mixture through a fine sieve into a small bowl. Press down hard on the herbs with the back of a spoon before you discard them. Return the wine to the saucepan, add the stock, and bring to a boil. Set the pan aside.

Cream butter by beating it briskly against the sides of a small bowl with a wooden spoon until it is fluffy. Beat in lemon juice, flour, and parsley. Set the bowl aside.

Steak
1 – 1½ lb. (500 – 750g) sirloin or other high quality steak, 1 inch thick and trimmed of excess fat
1 tbsp. (15ml) butter
1 tbsp. (15ml) vegetable oil
Freshly ground pepper to taste

Preheat oven to 220° F (100°C).

Pat the meat dry with paper towels. Cut small incisions every inch or so around the steak so it won't curl when cooked.

Melt butter and oil in a large skillet over high heat. Add meat and brown for 1 – 2 minutes per side. Reduce heat to moderate and continue to cook, 5 minutes per side, or until it's done to medium-rare. Turn meat only once.

Test steak by either making a small cut to check color or pressing on the steak with your finger. It should be slightly resilient, not soft nor firm. Transfer the meat to a platter, season with pepper, and place in the oven.

Pour wine mixture into skillet. Bring to a boil over moderate heat. Stir constantly and scrape in any browned bits from the pan sides and bottom. Remove from heat and stir in creamed butter mixture 2 tablespoons (25g) at a time so it blends well into the sauce.

To serve, divide the steak in half and drizzle on the sauce.

Direct from Merry Olde England is a tasty way to use those bits of beef you have frozen and promised yourself to reheat before they ended in the trash. This recipe works well with all types of beef and pork, or a combination of the two. Be sure to include any of the juices that have collected in your container.

Make the mashed potatoes first so everything is set to go when you assemble the pie.

Serve with Tossed Salad, and Cold Beer.

SHEPHERD'S PIE

Filling
2 tbsp. (30ml) olive oil
1 tbsp. (15ml) butter
1 large onion, chopped fine
1 large carrot, chopped fine
3 garlic cloves, pressed or chopped fine
1½ lbs. (750g) leftover meat, chopped bite size or smaller
4 sprigs rosemary, leaves removed or 1 tsp. (5ml) dried

4 sprigs thyme, leaves removed or 1 tsp. (5ml) dried
Freshly ground pepper to taste
2 tsp. (10ml) Worcestershire sauce
½ 6 oz. can (170g) tomato paste, freeze the remainder in a baggy for another recipe
¼ cup (60ml) dry red wine
½ cup (120ml) beef stock

Pour oil into a hot Dutch oven (you'll need this size pot so you have room to work) and stir in butter. Sauté onion and carrot until onion is translucent and tender, but not brown, 5 - 7 minutes.

Add garlic and stir for 60 seconds.

Combine meat, herbs, and pepper in the pot.

After each of these ingredients is added stir well; Worcestershire sauce, tomato paste, and red wine. Cook 2 minutes.

Pour stock into pan and heat through 3 minutes.

You don't have to be adamant on all the times. They are merely guides so you don't rush the process.

Mashed Potatoes
5 russet potatoes, peeled and coarsely chopped
¼ cup (115g) sour cream
¼ cup (60ml) milk
3½ tbsp. (50g) soft butter
1 egg yolk
Freshly ground pepper to taste
½ cup (57g) Parmesan cheese, maybe a little more for topping

Pour potatoes into a saucepan. Fill with water to cover them by an inch or so. Cover and bring to a boil. Cook until fork tender. Drain pan.

Add sour cream, some milk, all the butter, and pepper to the pan. Mash potatoes well. Add small amounts of milk until you achieve the consistency you prefer. Add egg yolk and half the Parmesan cheese. Stir well.

Cover with aluminum foil to keep from drying out until you assemble the pie.

Assemble the Pie
Preheat oven to 400° F (200°C).

Scoop meat into deep individual ovenproof bowls or a casserole dish. I prefer the individual bowls as this recipe freezes well or will hold in the refrigerator up to 4 days. Fill bowls no more than ¾ full.

Spoon mashed potatoes over the top and spread to the edges. This can be a little tricky. Don't press down on the spoon or the juice will flood over the potatoes. Sprinkle with a generous portion of Parmesan cheese.

Set bowls on a cookie sheet to protect the oven should they boil over. Bake 20 minutes or so to lightly brown the potatoes and set the pie.

If you use the individual bowls, serve them on dinner plates to protect your tabletop from the heat. The pie is extremely hot. Be sure to warn your diners so no one burns their mouth.

Studs and I plant a small vegetable garden every year. September is exciting because that's when the peppers (red, yellow, and green) are ready to pick. One of my favorite dishes to make is stuffed peppers based on an old Hungarian recipe. Be sure to make extras for another meal. The peppers freeze and reheat beautifully.

Serve with Boiled Potatoes, Polish Style Cucumber Salad, and Red Wine – Pinot Noir.

STUFFED PEPPERS

TÖLTÖTT PAPRIKA

6 med. – lg. peppers in any color you like
¾ cup (90g) rice
2 tbsp. (30ml) olive oil or lard
1 large onion, chopped
2 garlic cloves, pressed or chopped fine
1 lb. (500g) ground chuck/beef
1 lb. (500g) ground pork
1 egg lightly beaten
Freshly ground pepper to taste
1 tbsp. (15ml) dried parsley
1 tbsp. (15ml) vinegar

Cut tops off peppers and clean out seeds and ribs. Drop peppers into a pot of boiling water that completely covers them. Boil briskly 2 – 3 minutes. Cover pot, remove from heat and set aside for 5 minutes. With tongs or a slotted spoon, carefully remove peppers from the water and invert onto paper towels to drain.

Cook rice according to package directions, but only 10 minutes. Drain rice in a colander, run under cold water, and set aside.

Add olive oil or lard to a 10 inch skillet. Melt over medium heat until a light haze forms. Sauté onions until soft and translucent, 5 – 7 minutes. Do not let them brown. Drain well. Add garlic the last minute of cooking.

In a large bowl combine all ingredients. Mix well, cover, and set bowl in the refrigerator until you're ready to complete the recipe.

You can prepare the peppers up to this point three hours or so before baking. If you do, cover them with cling wrap and refrigerate. Set the chilled dish on the counter 1 hour before you complete the recipe so the meat cooks properly.

Sauce
1 cup (250ml) chicken stock, fresh or canned
2 tbsp. (30ml) flour
1 – 14 oz. can (411g) diced tomatoes
¼ cup (60ml) white vinegar

Preheat oven to 350° F (180°C).

Pour ¾ cup (200ml) chicken stock into a saucepan and heat over medium heat. Pour the remaining chicken stock in a small bowl. Sprinkle in the flour while stirring well with a whisk or fork. Whisk this mixture into the saucepan, stirring constantly. Cook over high heat until sauce comes to a boil. Reduce heat to low, simmer 3 minutes, stir in tomatoes with their liquid and vinegar. Heat through. Remove from heat.

Pour ¼ cup (60ml) or so of the sauce into an ovenproof baking dish that holds the peppers comfortably.

Spoon the meat mixture into the peppers, forming a small mound on top. DO NOT PACK THEM. Stand them in the baking dish. Shape the excess meat into medium-sized balls and lay between the peppers. Pour remaining sauce over meat.

Bake covered 30 minutes. Bake uncovered 10 – 15 minutes longer.

Rumor has it that over a century ago the Italian Working Girls prepared this dish for their late night customers from standard kitchen supplies. It was an added bonus for their clients and an easy way to keep business flowing. No matter how the name came to be, the dish is superb and freezes well.

**Serve with Caesar Salad, Italian Bread,
Olive Oil for dipping the bread, and Red Wine – Chianti.**

WHORE'S SPAGHETTI

PASTA PUNTENESCA

Sauce
¼ cup (60ml) olive oil
3 cloves garlic, minced
1 – 14.5 oz. can (411g) Italian plum tomatoes, drained and coarsely chopped
1 tbsp. (15ml) capers, chopped
1 can pitted black olives, drained and chopped
½ tsp. (2.5ml) red pepper flakes

1 tsp. (5ml) dried basil
1 tsp. (5ml) dried oregano
Freshly ground pepper to taste

Heat oil in a large saucepan over medium heat. Add garlic, stir 2 – 3 minutes.

Stir in tomatoes, capers, olives, pepper flakes, basil, and oregano. Turn heat to low, and simmer 15 minutes.

Add pepper. Taste the sauce, adjust seasoning to suit you.

Reduce heat to low, simmer another 15 minutes.

Pasta
1 lb. (454g) spaghetti
1 tsp. (5ml) fresh or dried parsley
Freshly grated Parmesan cheese

Cook spaghetti according to package directions until al dente.

Toss pasta with the sauce, sprinkle on parsley.

Serve with plenty of Parmesan cheese on the side.

SALAD

ASIAN SALAD

Dressing
¾ cup (200ml) olive oil
¼ cup (60ml) cider vinegar
¾ cup (90g) sugar
1 tbsp. (15ml) Worcestershire sauce
⅓ cup (75ml) ketchup
pinch salt
1 small onion, chopped

Beat all ingredients together well in a small bowl.

Salad
½ lb. (250g) bacon, chopped and fried crisp
1 lb. (500g) mixed lettuces, use a variety for more texture and taste
3 hard boiled eggs, chopped
1 can bean sprouts, drained
1 can water chestnuts, drained and sliced

Toss all the ingredients in a large bowl.

Refrigerate until meal time. Pour on dressing and toss right before you serve.

Scale this recipe down to suit the number of people you will serve as it goes limp by the next day.

CAESAR SALAD for TWO

1 egg, coddled
1 lg. clove garlic
½ tsp. (2.5ml) anchovy paste
Freshly ground pepper to taste
1 tbsp. (15ml) lemon juice, preferably fresh
3 drops white vinegar or as close to as possible
¼ cup (60ml) olive oil
Romaine lettuce, 3 leaves per person, washed and dried
½ cup (37g) Parmesan cheese, grated
1 bag croutons, optional

Remove egg from refrigerator well before assembling all the other ingredients on your counter. Eggs cook better for any recipe when close to room temperature.

Fill a small saucepan with water and bring to a boil. Place egg in water and boil 2 minutes. This process is called coddling. Rinse under cold water, crack shell, and then scoop the runny egg into a small bowl. Break up the solid white pieces and lightly mix. Later, you will add some of this to the salad dressing.

In a large glass or wooden serving bowl, mash the garlic with a spoon and fork into coarse pieces. Rub the pieces against the sides of the bowl to spread the oil they have released.

Add anchovy and pepper. Mix well. Pour in lemon juice and vinegar. Mix well. Add in ½ – ¾ of the coddled egg. Mix well. Blend in olive oil until the dressing thickens. Remove this mixture from your bowl and set aside to use right before serving.

Tear lettuce into bite size pieces. Add to salad bowl. Pour in some of the dressing. Toss well. Add more dressing if the lettuce looks too dry. Sprinkle on ¼ cup (28g) or so of Parmesan. Toss again.

Arrange salad on individual chilled bowls or plates. Sprinkle with remaining Parmesan and croutons. Serve immediately.

LEAFY GREENS with
CREAMY GARLIC SALAD DRESSING

Salad
Red leaf lettuce, 2 leaves per person
Romaine lettuce, 2 leaves per person
Head lettuce, 2 leaves per person
Tomato, 1 per 2 people
Crumbled Feta cheese, optional

Tear lettuces into a bowl. Chop tomato into bite size pieces and then add to lettuces. Cover with a damp paper towel and store in the refrigerator until ready to serve.

Dressing
1½ cups (350ml) mayonnaise – it must be real mayo
Scant ½ cup (100ml) vegetable oil
Scant ¼ cup (50ml) white vinegar
3 tbsp. (45ml) onion, chopped
4 lg. garlic cloves, pressed or chopped fine
¾ tsp. (3.75ml) sugar
¼ tsp. (1.25ml) salt

Combine all ingredients, except cheese, in a blender or food processor. Mix on high until smooth.

To serve, either toss lettuce with dressing or arrange salad on individual chilled plates and then ladle a dollop of dressing on top. In either case, freely sprinkle Feta across the top or lay a decent size chunk on the side.

The dressing stays good in fridge one month. It also tastes great slathered on hamburgers.

My grandmother learned this recipe from her mother when she was a girl in Poland. Grandma passed it on to my mother who prepared it every time she served sausage for dinner. It also tastes good with most types of sandwiches.

POLISH STYLE CUCUMBER SALAD

MIZERIA

1 cucumber, peeled and sliced paper thin
1 tsp. (5ml) salt
½ cup (115g) sour cream
Juice of ½ lemon
½ tsp. (2.5ml) sugar
¼ onion, sliced thin
½ tsp. (2.5ml) dried dill
¼ tsp. (1.25ml) pepper
Snipped chives, optional

Place cucumber slices in a colander. Sprinkle salt across the top. Allow to sit while you make the sauce.

Combine sour cream, lemon, sugar, onion, and dill in a medium-sized bowl.

Gently squeeze the moisture from the cucumber. Stir into sauce. Dust on, do not stir, pepper and chives.

Set in a cool place until ready to serve.

SNAZZY TOMATO SALAD

1 tomato per two people, cut in half and sliced ½ inch (1.25cm) thick
½ tbsp. (10ml) red wine vinegar
½ small onion, sliced medium-thin
1 tbsp. (15ml) fresh or dried chives

Prepare this dish at least an hour before serving.

Arrange tomatoes on a serving plate.

Drizzle vinegar over the tomatoes, then cast on onions. Sprinkle plenty of chives across the top.

Don't refrigerate. Set on the salad counter away from sun or heat to flavor through.

TASTY TOMATO SALAD

1 small plum or Roma tomato per person
½ cup (120ml) olive oil
2 tbsp. (30ml) red wine vinegar
1 tbsp. (15ml) finely cut fresh basil or 1 tsp. (5ml) dried
¼ tsp. (1.25ml) garlic, chopped fine
Freshly ground pepper to taste
2 tbsp. (30ml) scallions/green onions, sliced thin, be sure to include the green
1 tsp. (5ml) parsley, dried – if you use fresh, chop fine

Slice tomatoes ¼ inch (.6cm) thick. Arrange them in slightly overlapping concentric circles on a deep dish or platter.

Prepare the dressing by blending oil, vinegar, basil, garlic, and pepper in a small bowl. Spoon the mixture over the tomatoes.

Combine the scallions/green onions and parsley, then sprinkle evenly over the top.

Set salad on the counter away from sun and heat until you're ready to serve. Leftovers do not work well. The tomatoes become limp.

TOMATO & CUCUMBER SALAD

1 plum or Roma tomato per person
¼ cucumber per person
Freshly ground pepper to taste
Snipped chives to taste

Early in the day quarter tomatoes and then cut in half. Swipe tomatoes into a serving bowl.

Peel cucumber. Chop into ½ inch (1.25cm) bite size pieces. Mix with tomatoes.

Sprinkle on pepper and chives. Stir well.

Cover with cling wrap. Set on your counter away from the sun and heat until you're ready to serve.

Dive your hands right into the bowl and have fun with this no measuring allowed recipe. Select at least two types of lettuce. Let your creativity soar. Clean out the fridge by tossing in cut up radishes, carrots, zucchini, black olives, a few cheese cubes, and anything else that excites your taste buds.

TOSSED SALAD

Lettuce, torn into bite size pieces, green leaf and head are excellent
Tomatoes, sliced into wedges
Cucumber, unpeeled and sliced ¼ inch (.6cm) thick
Scallions/green onions, sliced, be sure to include some of the green
Mushrooms, sliced

Mix all ingredients together with your bare hands, but not the dressing, in a large bowl. Cover with a damp paper towel, and pop in the fridge until ready to serve.

Drizzle with **Rosemary Flavored Olive Oil** or your favorite bottled dressing. Anything works great with this easy salad. Pour on a small amount of dressing and toss. Or, set a variety of bottled dressings on the table for everyone to help themselves.

WARM ENDIVE & PINE NUT SALAD

1 tbsp. (15ml) Dijon mustard
1 tbsp. (15ml) red wine vinegar
½ tbsp. (7.5ml) lemon juice
3 tbsp. (45ml) extra-virgin olive oil, or as needed
Freshly ground pepper to taste
4 heads Belgian endive
⅓ cup (40g) pine nuts
1 tbsp. (15ml) chopped fresh parsley, optional

In a medium bowl, whisk together mustard, vinegar, and lemon juice. Whisk in olive oil slowly until you have an almost creamy consistency. Taste and season with pepper. Set aside.

Cut endive heads crosswise into rings. Remove the hard ends of the stems and discard. Rinse in a colander, shaking to separate the slices into rings. Set aside to drain.

Toast pine nuts in a frying pan over medium heat. Stir constantly so that they do not burn. Once the nuts are golden, add the endive rings. Warm slightly, then pour in the dressing and toss to coat. Reduce heat a bit if the endive is wilting too quickly. You want to maintain some crispness and texture.

If you want to impress someone special, sprinkle on parsley. The sharp green flecks will brighten the dish and enhance the flavor, but the salad is in no way lacking without it.

Serve immediately.

REMOULADE SAUCE

⅓ cup (40g) scallions/green onions, sliced
¼ cup (30g) celery, chopped fine
1 large glove garlic, chopped fine
1½ tbsp. (20ml) fresh parsley, chopped
1 tsp. (5ml) capers, drained, chopped
½ tbsp. (7.5ml) horseradish
1½ tbsp. (20ml) whole grain mustard
½ tbsp. (7.5ml) prepared mustard
1 tbsp. (15ml) ketchup
½ tbsp. (7.5ml) Worchester sauce
1 tsp. (5ml) Frank's hot sauce or ¼ tsp. (.60ml) Tabasco sauce
½ tbsp. (7.5ml) lemon juice
½ tsp. (2.5ml) paprika
Freshly ground pepper to taste
1 cup, (100g) mayonnaise, no imitations

Place all ingredients except mayonnaise in a food processor. Process until semi-smooth. Scrape down the sides. Continue to process until smooth, 30 – 45 seconds in all.

Add mayonnaise. Blend well.

Pour sauce into a serving dish, cover, and refrigerate until dinner.

Keeps well in your fridge up to 3 months.

TARTAR SAUCE

1 cup (100g) real mayonnaise, no imitations
2 small garlic clove, chopped fine
2 tbsp. (30ml) onion, chopped fine
2 tbsp. (30ml) sweet relish

Mix ingredients together in a small bowl. Taste and adjust to your preference.

Cover and refrigerate until ready to serve.

Stores well in the fridge for 3 weeks.

HOMEMADE APPLESAUCE

6 lg. apples, cored, peeled, and coarsely sliced*
1 cup (100g) sugar
4 tbsp. (60ml) water
2 tbsp. (30ml) lemon juice
1½ tbsp. (21g) soft butter

Combine all ingredients, except butter, in a saucepan. Bring to a boil over medium heat. Reduce heat, cover pot, and simmer 15 – 20 minutes or until apples mash easily with a fork.

Remove pan from the heat. Stir in butter.

Crush apples with a potato masher. For a smoother texture pour sauce into a blender or food processor and puree 1 minute.

Turn into a serving bowl, cover, and refrigerate until ready to serve. This recipe also freezes well.

*Mix it up with a variety of apples to improve the flavor by using six different types.

SAGE BUTTERED PASTA

8 tbsp. (1 stick) (114g) butter, room temperature
6 – 10 sage leaves
2 cups (240g) curly pasta
Freshly grated Parmesan cheese

Cook pasta according to package directions. Set aside while you make the sauce.

Melt butter in a frying pan over medium heat.

Add sage. Allow butter to brown. Watch carefully and stir often as once this starts to brown it can quickly burn. Cook until butter reaches a medium caramel color. Remove sage leaves and discard.

Stir in pasta. Be sure to coat noodles well. Heat through. Serve with plenty of Parmesan cheese.

Spätzle, which translates to "little sparrow" because that's what the dough looks like after it's pressed, is a marvelous noodle renowned in Germany and Austria since 1725. It works well with roasted meats and poultry, as well as sausages. Gravy, sauce, or just a smear of butter is a perfect addition to this side dish.

SPÄTZLE

1 cup (120g) all-purpose flour
½ tsp. (2.5ml) salt
½ tsp. (2.5ml) ground nutmeg
Pinch white pepper*
2 eggs, lightly beaten
¼ cup (60ml) milk
8 tbsp. (1 stick) (114g) butter
2 tbsp. (30ml) fresh parsley, chopped

Bring 2 quarts (2L) of water to a boil in a large saucepan.

While the water is heating, combine flour, salt, nutmeg, and pepper in a medium-sized bowl.

Pour milk into a small bowl, add eggs, and stir well. Pour this mixture into the flour slowly, stir constantly. Continue to stir until you've created a smooth dough.

Set a colander, preferably one with large holes, over boiling water. Press dough, a few tablespoons at a time, directly into the water. Gently stir spätzle after each addition so they don't stick together. Boil briskly 5 – 8 minutes or until tender. Drain thoroughly.

You can stop here. Cover the spätzle so it doesn't dry out and leave on the counter.

To serve, melt butter in a large frying pan. Add spätzle and warm through. Swipe the noodles into a serving dish and then sprinkle on parsley.

*No need to buy white pepper if you don't have it. Use black pepper, but a little more as it is not as strong as the white.

Prepare this recipe a day or two in advance of cooking when your time is tight. Stop at the baking point, cover with foil, and refrigerate or freeze for future meals.

STUFFING

1 package bread stuffing cubes, plain or seasoned
½ lb. (250g) breakfast sausage in a tube or bulk
8 tbsp. (1 stick) (114g) butter, melted
1 rib celery, chopped
½ medium onion, chopped
1 egg, lightly beaten
1½ tsp. (7.5ml) dried sage
1½ tsp. (7.5ml) dried thyme
2 cups (450ml) chicken stock, maybe a little more

Empty bread cubes into a large bowl.

Fry sausage in a medium-sized skillet, breaking meat into small chunks, until no longer pink. Add sausage and its juice to bread cubes.

Melt butter in same skillet. Add celery and onion when the foam subsides. Sauté 3 – 4 minutes until translucent, be careful not to let it brown. Add vegetables with all their juices to the bread cubes. Mix well.

Pour egg onto stuffing. Sprinkle sage and thyme across the top. Mix well.

Stir in chicken stock until mixture is very moist, but not soupy.

To Bake as a Side Dish
Spoon mixture into an ungreased baking dish. Do not pack it in. Cover tightly with foil. Refrigerate stuffing until you are ready to bake it, but no longer than two days.

To Freeze
Spoon the mixture into freezer bags, label, and pop in freezer no longer than 3 months. I use several small bags that will serve 2 at a single setting.

No matter which route you take, remove stuffing from the refrigerator/freezer early in the day to allow it to come to room temperature.

Preheat oven to 350° F (180°C). Bake for a half hour. Remove foil and continue to bake until the top is brown.

CREAMY GARLIC SALAD DRESSING

1½ cups (350ml) mayonnaise – it must be real mayo
Scant ½ cup (100ml) vegetable oil
Scant ¼ cup (50ml) white vinegar
3 tbsp. onion, chopped
4 lg. cloves garlic, pressed or chopped fine
¾ tsp. (3.75ml) sugar
¼ tsp. (1.25ml) salt
Feta cheese, crumbled or chunk, optional

Combine all ingredients, except cheese, in a blender or food processor. Mix on high until smooth.

To serve either toss lettuce with dressing or arrange salad on individual chilled plates and then ladle a dollop of dressing on top. In either case, freely sprinkle Feta across the top or lay a decent sized chunk on the side.

The dressing stays good in fridge one month. It also tastes great slathered on hamburgers.

This is a wonderful salad dressing that can also be used to sauté vegetables or fry meat and poultry.

ROSEMARY INFUSED OIL

Good quality olive oil
Sprigs of fresh rosemary

Slip several sprigs of rosemary into a glass bottle. Pour in oil. Be sure herbs are covered completely with the oil.

Set the bottle on your counter, away from the sun, for three days. Remove herbs and discard. The flavored oil is good for two months.

This method works well with all herbs and/or garlic.

·

VEGGIES

STEAMED ASPARAGUS

1 bunch asparagus
½ cup (120ml) chicken stock
¼ cup (60ml) dry vermouth or white wine
Water
2 tbsp. (25g) butter
Metal vegetable steamer

Add chicken stock and dry vermouth or wine to a medium-sized saucepan. Insert vegetable steamer, then add water to just below the bottom holes.

Trim asparagus spears to fit your steamer. Lay them in the pan and cover it. Bring to a boil over medium heat and then adjust heat to a strong simmer. In 4 – 5 minutes the asparagus should be crisp tender.

Place asparagus in a serving dish. Spread butter over them and serve.

White asparagus are a treasured fresh vegetable in Germany. The freshest crop is available from May through most of the summer. They do have a tough skin and require a little extra work to prepare, but the end result is well worth the work.

WHITE ASPARAGUS

6 cups (1.5L) water
1 tbsp. (15ml) lemon juice
3 tbsp. (45ml) butter
1 lb. (500g) white asparagus
Extra butter for serving

Bring water, juice, and butter to a simmer in a pot set over medium heat.

Lay spears on a cutting board. Cut off ½ inch (1.25cm) or so of the stems. Starting 1½ inches (3.8cm) from the top of the spear, trim off a thin sliver down the length of the asparagus with a vegetable peeler. Do this all around the spear. Spears are brittle so be sure to lay them flat or they will break apart.

Place trimmed spears in simmering water. Be sure to maintain a simmer, not a boil, no matter how high you need to raise the heat. Cook until tender, 8 – 30 minutes depending on thickness of the asparagus. Test for doneness with the tip of a sharp knife. It should insert easily but not go through the spear.

Arrange spears in a serving dish and dot with butter.

Fresh broccoli is sold as heads and crowns. The difference is the length of thick stalk left on the broccoli when sold. Heads have it all whereas crowns have a minimal amount. Crowns are a better value for your money since you have much less stalk to throw away. So what are florets, you ask? Easy. Broccoli turns into florets when you cut it up to cook. The longer the stem you leave after chopping off the thick stalk, the larger the floret clusters when you separate the tender stems. The shorter the stem left on, which means you cut the vegetable closer to each individual head, the more little trees or florets you gain. Both methods are good. It's purely a matter of the cook's taste.

BROCCOLI FLORETS

1 broccoli head or crown
¾ cup (200ml) chicken stock fresh or canned
Tap water
2 tbsp. (30ml) butter
Freshly ground pepper to taste
Metal vegetable steamer

Rinse and trim broccoli into florets.

Pour chicken stock into a saucepan. Add vegetable steamer and water to just below the bottom holes. Lay in broccoli. Cover and maintain a simmer until broccoli is tender, 3 – 4 minutes. The florets should have a little crunch to them.

If you don't have a steamer, drop broccoli into the simmering water mixture. Cover and cook until just tender, 3 – 4 minutes.

Carefully spoon broccoli into a serving bowl, dot with butter, and then add pepper.

SAUTÉED BROCCOLI

1 broccoli head or crown
3 tbsp. (45ml) olive oil, possibly a little more
2 tbsp. (25g) butter
1 clove garlic, pressed or chopped fine
¼ cup (28g) Parmesan cheese

Cut broccoli segments from the stem. Discard stem.

Preheat a frying pan over medium heat. Pour in olive oil, then add butter. When the foam subsides, add broccoli pieces, turn them to coat well with the oil and butter. You may need a little more oil. Be careful not to add too much.

Add garlic on top of broccoli. Sauté until just tender, 4 – 6 minutes. You want a little crisp left in the spears.

Sprinkle with Parmesan cheese and serve.

My niece has a wonderful kitchen with plenty of light, counter space, and a large island that holds her cook top. It's the perfect location to test new ideas and fine tune family favorites.

She decided to create a delicious Brussels sprout dish while I worked magic on a pot of fresh green beans. Give our recipes a try. I think you'll enjoy them both.

TRULY YUMMY BRUSSELS SPROUTS

1 lb. (500g) fresh Brussels sprouts
6 strips bacon, chopped
½ medium onion, diced
8 tbsp. (1 stick) (114g) butter or margarine
Freshly ground pepper to taste

Trim stems off sprouts and remove any tough outer leaves and stem. Slice sprouts in half lengthwise if they are large.

Set a large skillet over medium heat. Fry bacon until lightly browned. Add butter, onions, and sprouts. Cook until veggies are tender, 5 – 10 minutes. Stir frequently.

Sprinkle with pepper and serve.

CANDIED CARROTS

½ lb. (250g) packaged mini carrots
Juice from 1 medium orange
1 pinch nutmeg
¼ cup (60ml) maple syrup
4 tbsp. (57g) butter
Fresh parsley, chopped

Combine ingredients, except parsley, in a saucepan. Cover and gently simmer until carrots are bright orange and tender.

Garnish with the parsley and serve.

FRESH GREEN BEANS

10 beans per person, ends snapped off
Tap water
3 tbsp. (43g) butter per 20 beans
Freshly ground pepper to taste

Fill a medium-sized saucepan with cold water. Leave enough room to add beans. Cover pot and set on the stove over medium-high heat. Bring to a full boil. Drop beans in by the handful. Return water to a boil, reduce heat to moderate and boil beans uncovered for 8 – 12 minutes or until they are just tender. Drain and return beans to the pot.

If beans are to be served immediately, melt butter in the cooking pot and toss the beans for a minute or two. Season with pepper, then transfer beans to a heated dish and serve.

If serving the beans later, refresh them after draining by plunging the colander into a large pot of cold water for a minute or two. Drain thoroughly, cover and set aside. Refrigerate if they are to be used the next day. When ready to serve, melt butter, toss beans, and warm them over moderate heat.

SAUTÉED MUSHROOMS

8 oz. (250g) mini bella mushrooms
1 tbsp. (15ml) olive oil
½ small onion, sliced thin
2 tbsp. (25g) butter
2 tbsp. (30ml) dry vermouth or white wine
Freshly ground pepper to taste

Clean mushrooms with a paper towel to remove bedding soil. Slice them in half lengthwise if medium or into thirds if large.

Over medium heat dribble a small amount of olive oil into a medium-sized frying pan and add butter. Stir in onions and mushrooms. Sauté until almost tender, 3 – 6 minutes.

Pour vermouth or white wine over the mushrooms and continue to heat.

To serve, grind pepper across the top and spoon into a warm serving dish.

This dish is best cooked and served on the same day. Leftovers are soggy.

BAKED POTATOES

1 russet potato per person
Olive oil
Aluminum foil
Butter
Sour cream
Chives
Freshly ground pepper to taste

Preheat oven to 400° F (200°C).

Wash potatoes under cool water. Pat dry. Poke several sets of holes in each potato with a fork. This stops the potato from bursting as it bakes.

Rub potatoes with a small amount of olive oil to keep the skin soft.

Wrap each potato in a section of foil. Lay them on a cookie sheet. Bake 50 – 70 minutes or until a toothpick inserted in the potato shows no resistance.

Remove foil and then cut an X across the top of each potato. Using potholders squeeze the ends toward the center until the potato puffs up.

Serve with butter, sour cream, chives, and pepper.

BOILED POTATOES

1 red potato per person, peeled and quartered
Chicken stock
Tap water
1 lg. bay leaf
Freshly ground pepper to taste
Butter to taste

Add potatoes to a saucepan that holds them comfortably. Pour stock halfway up the potatoes. Top off with water, covering potatoes by an inch (2.5cm) or so. Add bay leaf. Set a lid on top.

You can do up to this point earlier in the day. Leave on the counter or stovetop until you are ready to cook.

Bring to a boil over medium heat. Adjust the lid and heat so the water continues a soft/light boil, but does not spill over. Cook 15 – 20 minutes, then test for doneness. A fork will insert easily.

Drain potatoes and discard bay leaf. Sprinkle pepper over potatoes. Add butter. Stir carefully so as not to smash potatoes.

Don't have bay leaf? Add 1 tablespoon (15ml) or so of dried basil to the pot. When you drain the potatoes most of the leaves will be gone, but the good taste remains.

CHEESY SCALLOPED POTATOES

1 large garlic clove, peeled and bruised with the flat of a knife
1 – 2 tbsp. (15 – 25g) butter for baking dish
5 red potatoes, peeled and sliced thin
1½ cups (170g) Swiss cheese, grated
6 tbsp. (85g) butter, cut into small bits
Freshly ground black pepper to taste
1 cup (250ml) heavy cream

Preheat oven to 450° F (230°C).

Rub the bottom and sides of a medium-sized baking dish with garlic. Grease dish lightly with butter.

Dry potato slices between paper towels. Spread half of them on the bottom of the dish. Sprinkle with half the cheese and butter bits. Grind pepper across the top.

Spread remaining potato slices in the dish followed by cheese, butter, and pepper. Pour cream down the side of the dish.

Bake in the upper third of the oven 25 minutes or until the potatoes are almost tender when pierced with a sharp knife. Remove any residual liquid with a bulb baster. Bake another 5 – 10 minutes until potatoes are tender, the cream absorbed, and the top is nicely browned.

HOMEMADE FRIES

1 Idaho potato per person
2 – 3 cups (450 – 750ml) vegetable oil
½ cup (104g) lard, optional
salt to taste

Wash potatoes under cool water. Peel, but it's not necessary. Cut potatoes in half lengthwise, then lay flat and slice into thirds. Place pieces in a bowl with enough water to cover them. Chill in the refrigerator for at least 2 hours.

Preheat oven to 220° F (100°C).

Heat oil and lard in a deep saucepan or skillet on medium-high. Test temperature by dropping in a piece of bread. When bread browns in a few seconds the oil is ready.

Drain potatoes then pat dry. Carefully add to hot oil. Deep-fry approximately 4 minutes. They're done when golden and a toothpick inserts easily.

Lay the fries on a plate lined with paper towels. Sprinkle on salt and then set the plate in the oven to keep warm while you finish the rest of the meal.

MASHED POTATOES

Chicken stock, not broth
1 small russet potato per person, peeled and quartered
3 tbsp. (43g) butter
Sour cream, a very large dollop
¼ cup (60ml) milk, at room temperature
Freshly ground pepper to taste
Parsley, snipped or chopped for garnish

Preheat oven to 220° F (100°C).

Pour one inch (2.5cm) chicken stock into saucepan. Place potatoes in saucepan. Add tap water to cover by one inch (2.5cm). Cover the pan and bring to a boil over medium heat. Lower temperature to a strong simmer. Cook approximately 20 - 25 minutes. Potatoes are done when a fork inserts easily into a section.

Drain potatoes. Stir in butter, sour cream, and pepper. Mash well. Drizzle in milk. Mash and continue to add milk until you achieve the consistency you prefer.

Keep the saucepan warm in the oven while you finish preparing dinner.

Viva la France!

Give this recipe direct from France a try. The potatoes have a delicate flavor and go well with any roasted or fried meat recipe.

PARSLEY POTATOES

POMMES DE TERRE PER SILLEES

3 tbsp. (43g) butter
2 white/russet potatoes, peeled and sliced thin
2 bay leaves
2 tbsp. (30ml) fresh parsley, chopped or 1 tbsp. (15ml) dried
Freshly ground pepper to taste
⅓ cup (75ml) cream or milk

Preheat oven to 375° F (190°C).

Coat the inside of an ovenproof dish with 1 – 1½ teaspoons (5 – 8g) of butter. Place a bay leaf on the bottom.

Cover with a layer of potatoes. Scatter parsley and pepper across the top. Continue this pattern until you use all the potatoes. Be sure to finish with just the potatoes. Lay the second bay leaf on top.

Pour the cream over the potatoes.

Bake uncovered 50 – 60 minutes or until potatoes are tender.

These potatoes are definitely out of the norm, but they are great with any meat dish.

ROASTED POTATOES

3 tbsp. (45ml) olive oil
3 tbsp. (45ml) cider vinegar
1 tbsp. (15ml) kosher salt
1 tsp. (5ml) dried thyme
1 red potato per person, quartered but not peeled

Preheat oven to 425° F (215°C).

In a small bowl whisk together the olive oil, vinegar, salt, and thyme.

Place the potatoes in a large plastic bag. Pour the mixture over them and gently shake the bag to coat evenly.

Spread potatoes in an even layer on a baking sheet. Drizzle remaining mixture over them. Bake until potatoes are toothpick tender and slightly browned, 50 – 60 minutes.

Here's an easy veggie that fits into everyone's busy schedule yet the presentation looks like you slaved for hours. An added bonus is that the potatoes can be made a day ahead of time and final baked when you're ready to serve.

TWICE BAKED POTATOES

1 baking potato per person
Olive oil
Butter
Extra sharp cheddar cheese, grated
Sour cream
Freshly ground pepper to taste
Paprika

The amounts of the ingredients are left up to your taste, but don't be sparing if you want great flavor.

Preheat oven to 400° F (200°C).

Wash potatoes under cool water. Pat dry. Rub skins with a little olive oil. Make a small slit across their tops. Lay on a cookie sheet. Bake 1 hour or until a toothpick is easily inserted.

Combine butter, cheddar cheese, sour cream, and pepper into a small bowl.

When potatoes are tender, lay them on a cutting board and slice them in half. They'll be very hot so use pot holders. Scoop the pulp into the above mixture. Be careful not to rip the skins. Whip the mixture well.

Refill the shells and set them back on a cookie sheet. Sprinkle with a little paprika for color.

**Stop here if you plan to serve the potatoes the next day. Cover with cling wrap and refrigerate. Remove from the refrigerator at least one hour before baking.

No matter which option you use, preheat reheat oven to 325° F (160°C).

Bake uncovered 25 – 30 minutes. You only want to heat the potatoes so don't overdo the baking time.

This recipe is best prepared a day in advance and then reheated. It also freezes well for future meals.

SAUERKRAUT

1 jar or bag sauerkraut
5 slices bacon, chopped
1 small onion, chopped
½ tsp. (2.5ml) ground thyme
2 cups (450ml) chicken stock, not broth

Preheat oven to 325° F (160°C).

Empty sauerkraut into a colander. Rinse under tap water several times. Squeeze out most of the moisture and fluff with a fork.

Fry bacon in a medium-sized saucepan over medium heat until crisp. Set pieces on a paper towel. Do not pour out grease rendered from the bacon.

Add onion to pan and sauté until translucent, 5 – 7 minutes. Do not brown the onion, it will be bitter. Be sure to scrape in all the bits that cling to the sides and bottom of the pan.

Return bacon to saucepan. Stir in sauerkraut. Sprinkle thyme over the mixture. Mix well. Cook 3 – 4 minutes over moderate heat.

Stir in stock. Cover and bake in the oven 30 minutes or until sauerkraut is tender, but still has crunch. This could take as long as 2 hours, depending on the brand you use. Add more stock if necessary to keep the sauerkraut moist.

If you make the kraut a day in advance, cover and refrigerate. Remove from fridge an hour before reheating in a 325° F (160°C) oven 30 minutes. Be sure to keep the sauerkraut moist by adding more chicken stock as needed.

Another amazing recipe from France you will want to serve often. Simply increase the ingredient amounts proportionally when you prepare this dish for company.

SNOW PEAS with LETTUCE & CHIVES

POIS MANGETOUT A LA FRANCAISE

4 oz. (125g) snow peas
2 tbsp. (25g) butter
Pinch of sugar
½ Boston lettuce, shredded
1 tbsp. (15ml) chives, chopped fine, or 1½ tsp. (7.5ml) dried
2 scallions/green onions, sliced fine, be sure to include the green stems

Trim ends off peas. Melt butter in a saucepan over medium heat. Be careful not to let this burn. When the foam subsides stir in peas. Stir in sugar. Cover and cook 5 minutes.

Add lettuce, chives, and onions. Gently toss until lettuce has wilted.

Scoop into a bowl and serve.

BAKED SWEET POTATOES

1 potato per person, rinsed but not scrubbed
Olive oil
Aluminum foil
Butter

Preheat oven to 400° F (200°CF).

Wash potatoes under cool water. Pat dry. Rub a little oil on potatoes to keep them supple while baking. Wrap potatoes individually in foil. Lay them on a cookie sheet.

Bake 50 minutes (depending on their size) or until a tooth pick inserts easily.

Serve with butter as you would a baked Idaho potato.

CONVERSION CHART

LIQUID		DRY					
Cup	**Metric**	**Ounces**	**Metric**		**Cup**	**Metric**	
¼ cup	60ml	4 oz. (¼ lb)	125g		¼ cup	30g	
⅓ cup	75ml	8 oz. (½ lb)	250g		⅓ cup	40g	
½ cup	120ml	16 oz. (1 lb)	500g (½kg)		½ cup	60g	
¾ cup	200ml	24 oz. (1 ½ lb)	750g		⅔ cup	75g	
1 cup	250ml	2 oz. (2 lb)	1kg		¾ cup	90g	
1½ cups	350ml	48 oz. (3 lb)	1.5kg		1 cup	100g	
2 cups	450ml	64 oz. (4 lb)	2kg		1½ cups	200g	
3 cups	750ml	76 oz. (5 lb)	2.5kg		2 cups	200g	
4 cups (1 qt.)	1L						

LIQUID		Cheese		BUTTER MEASURES	
Spoon	**Metric**	**Cups**	**Metric**	**Spoon**	**Metric**
⅛ tsp.	.60ml	¼ cup	28g	1 tbsp.	15g
¼ tsp.	1.25ml	⅓ cup	37g	1½ tbsp.	21g
½ tsp.	2.5ml	½ cup	57g	2 tbsp.	25g
¾ tsp.	3.75ml	1 cup	113g	3 tbsp.	43g
1 tsp.	5ml	1½ cups	170g	4 tbsp.-- ¼ cup	57g
1½ tsp.	7.5ml			6 tbsp.	85g
2 tsp.	10ml			8 tbsp.--1 stick--½ cup	114g
½ tbsp.	7.5ml				
1 tbsp.	15ml	**Solid Shortening**		**Pasta**	
1½ tbsp.	20ml	¼ cup	52g	2 cups	240g
2 tbsp.	30ml	½ cup	104g	½ lb	227g
3 tbsp.	45ml	1 cup	205g	1 lb	454g
4 tbsp.	60ml				
5 tbsp.	75ml				
6 tbsp.	90ml				

Fahrenheit	Celsius	Gas
220°	100°	
250°	120°	1
300°	150°	2 slow
325°	160°	3 moderately slow
350°	180°	4 moderate
375°	190°	5 moderately hot
400°	200°	6 hot
425°	220°	
450°	230°	7 very hot
500°	250°	9 super hot

COOKING TIPS

General

Always cook with a sink of hot soapy water at the ready. It makes cleanup easier.

Write the date and your opinion along with any adjustments on your recipes. Make a note in the index, i.e., VG (very good), etc. for future reference.

Sponges are a manmade cleaning treasure that is a breeding ground for bacteria. Discard your used sponge, no matter how clean it looks, monthly.

No one needs a whole sponge to do dishes. Cut the sponge into quarters. Use one now and save the remainder for the following month.

Meats

Do not flour roasts before you brown them. All you're browning is the flour and the meat is not sealed to hold in its juices.

Always allow roasts, steaks, etc. to sit on a cutting board for 10 minutes, with a foil tent over, before you carve it. This allows the juices to sink back into the meat.

Fruit

Avocado

Do not toss the pits when you make guacamole or another dip that uses avocados. Save them to plunge into the serving dish. The dip will stay green and fresh for at least two days.

Banana

The easiest method to peel a stubborn banana is from the bottom up. That's right, flip it end over end and strip away.

Cantaloupe

For the sweetest fruit, skip the smooth rinds, and look for the rinds that have cellulite-looking wrinkles.

Pineapple

The day prior to serving cut off the top. Turn the pineapple upside down on a plate and allow it to sit on your counter. All the beautiful juices return to the cut end and make the entire pineapple more flavorful.

Strawberries

What you see is what you get. Strawberries are the only fruit that does not ripen more once it is picked. Those big white sections you see in the plastic container are with you forever.

You can store fresh strawberries in the refrigerator for up to four days. Do not wash them. Lay a paper towel on a plate or low dish, then add the strawberries, but do not mound them. Wash when ready to use.

Tomato

Place unripe tomatoes in a brown paper bag. Store in a cool dark spot. This is also great for all the green tomatoes you rescue from your garden at the end of summer.

Do not store tomatoes in the refrigerator. They lose their flavor.

Vegetables

Steam fresh vegetables to retain bright color and crispness. Place a metal steamer in your saucepan. Add chicken stock, white wine, and water to just below the bottom steamer holes. The stock and wine add a little extra flavor and the alcohol cooks away.

Dried and Canned Beans

When cooking beans for soup, stews, and the like, add a teaspoon or so of baking soda to the mixture. This cuts the negative intestinal reactions to beans and does not affect the flavor or cooking.

Fresh Green Beans

Add a paper towel to the plastic bag when you store green beans in the refrigerator. It absorbs the excess moisture so the beans stay fresh for a longer period of time.

Celery

What to do with those extra stalks that you don't need, but don't want to throw out at today's prices? Chop and sauté in a mix of olive oil and butter. Store in small containers, and freeze until needed for soups, stews, and the like.

If you have too much to cook up, still chop the stalks and then freeze them raw in a plastic bag. Simply grab your required amount for your recipe and cook away!

Garlic - Fresh

Use a garlic press instead of chopping. The press brings out more flavor and you'll use less garlic.

Lettuce

All types need moisture to stay fresh. When buying head lettuce, look for the longest stem. Scratch the nub with your nail, sprinkle with water, and place in an open plastic bag. Store in the fridge, preferably the crisper drawer.

Leaf lettuces should be rinsed in cool water, wrapped in a dish towel or other cloth, and stored in the crisper drawer of your fridge.

Remoisten the lettuce after each use to retain freshness.

Mushrooms

Clean mushrooms just before using. Wipe with a dry paper towel to remove the growing soil.

Loose mushrooms keep reasonably well in a paper bag and stored in the refrigerator.

After you use a portion of mushrooms that come in a plastic container, cover the remainder with cling wrap and store in the refrigerator.

Onions

Cut the root end off onions first. This allows the gas that makes your eyes water to escape.

What to do with the rest of an onion when the recipe calls for a small amount? Sauté the remainder. Freeze in small containers for your next recipe.

OR chop and freeze raw in a plastic bag. When you need a little onion for any cooked recipe, simply scoop out the required amount and toss it into the pot.

After you cut the roots off a green onion, use a piece of paper towel to pull off the slippery end. Stops your fingers from smelling and being sticky.

Salads

Make your salad early in the day and never worry about it turning brown or mushy. Add your salad ingredients, without the dressing, to a large bowl. Gently toss until well mixed. Cover with a damp paper towel and store in fridge until you're ready to add dressing and serve.

Herbs

Chop fresh herb leaves easily. Place the leaves, without stems, into a cup and snip with scissors.

Dairy

Cheese

Spray your cheese grater with a little non-stick cooking spray. The cheese won't stick and cleanup is a breeze.

Grate your own Parmesan, Asiago, Swiss, etc. fresh when you need it. The remainder of the block will keep in your fridge for months if you cover tightly with cling wrap or aluminum foil, then store in a plastic bag. Should a little mold appear simply scrape it off with a knife. Surprisingly the cheese is still good.

Eggs

Make hardboiled eggs easily. Eggs should be in your refrigerator no less than 5 days otherwise they are devils to peel. Set eggs in a saucepan and then fill with cold water to cover. Be sure to add the lid so the pan boils faster. Bring to a boil over medium heat. Turn off the burner and keep the pan on the burner for 8 - 9 minutes.

Peeling hard boiled eggs is easy. After the eggs are boiled, pour out the hot water. Add cold water to the pot. Crack the end of each egg against your sink gently, then place them back in the cold water while you do the others. Roll the eggs along the counter or the middle part of your sink with a little pressure. This takes a little practice to master so you don't mush the egg. The shell peels off easily.

Store peeled hardboiled eggs for up to five days in a glass container. Cover the eggs with water. Change the water every other day.

Milk

Children of any age should not drink expired milk, but adults can for an additional day or two without a problem.

Additional Tips

Bread

Don't store bread in the refrigerator. This dries it out.

Bread freezes well for up to one month.

Brown Sugar

When light or dark brown sugar hardens place it into a plastic bag. Add a slice of white bread and seal. Within hours the sugar is back to a usable state.

Cooking Oil

Test if the oil is hot enough for frying by adding a small piece of white bread to the heated pan. When the bread toasts golden quickly the oil is ready.

Test if the oil is hot enough for frying by adding a small piece of white bread to the heated pan. When the bread toasts golden quickly the oil is ready.

Ice Ring

The following recipe is simple and adds a festive look to any punch bowl.

Water
1 orange, peeled and sliced thin
10 maraschino cherries, halved
15 seedless red grapes, halved
10 strawberries, halved
25 blueberries

Arrange thin citrus slices and another fruit of your choice, or any combination of fruits omitting the orange, in an attractive design in a Bundt pan. Pour water into mold to partially cover fruit. Freeze.

When frozen, add water to fill mold ¾ full. Another option is to use orange juice, another juice, or ginger ale whichever works best with your recipe in place of water. This keeps the punch cold without diluting it. Refreeze.

At serving time, unmold by dipping the pan in hot water to loosen the ice. Float the ring fruit side up in punch bowl.

Pasta

Don't add oil or salt to the cooking water. Those additions make it difficult for the sauce to cling to the pasta.

Here's a handy trick my friend Bonnie learned from her dad Frank. After pasta is cooked *al dente* and drained, return it to the pot. Stir in a few ladles of hot sauce. Allow to sit for a few minutes before serving. This stops the watery ring that forms on your dinner plate or bowl.

PHOTO CREDITS

ABOUT THE AUTHOR

Sloane Taylor is an award-winning author with a second passion in her life. She is an avid cook and creator of new recipes. Every Wednesday she posts a recipe on SloaneTaylor.com that is user friendly, meaning easy. This cookbook is Taylor's first solo venture into non-fiction.

Taylor was born and raised on the Southside of Chicago. She and her husband now live in a small home in Northwest Indiana and enjoy the change from city life.

Also by Sloane Taylor

NAUGHTY LADIES OF NICE Series

French Tart
French Delight
French Twist
French Kiss
French Tickler

BOX SET

Naughty Ladies of Nice

STAND ALONE NOVELLA

Photo Op!

FREE COMPILED COOKBOOKS

ABCDs of Cooking with Writers
Sweets & Treats for Someone Special

Made in the USA
Middletown, DE
13 December 2020